GRAFTERS

Behind the Scenes

GRAFTERS
Behind the Scenes

Douglas Thompson

GRANADA
MEDIA

First published in 1999
by Granada Media, an imprint of André Deutsch Ltd,
in association with Granada Media Group
76 Dean Street
London
W1V 5HA
www.vci.co.uk

A catalogue record for this book is available from the British Library

ISBN 0 233 99723 7

Design by Whitelight
Printed and bound in the UK by Jarrold Book Printing

1 3 5 7 9 10 8 6 4 2

Photographs by Nicky Johnston are on pages: 1, 9, 10, 13, 28, 48, 59, 75, 84, 122, 125

CONTENTS

*'He ain't heavy, Father,
he's my brother'*

– Mickey Rooney, *Boys' Town*, 1938

PROLOGUE
HIGH TIDE

'I do like to be beside the seaside'
— traditional song

Not long after dawn, as a bitter April wind makes the sun play hide-and-seek with the clouds, a couple of figures are bravely tramping along the tightly packed sand of Shoreham Beach.

One is tall and rangy in white T-shirt and jeans, leaning into the strong sea breeze. The other is wrapped in a black leather jacket, but his dinky blue denim shorts expose the goosebumps on his knees. There is an intense discussion and then the two whirl around, like contestants in a duel, and pace off. Then, hitting specific spots in the sand, they turn and march at each other, perfectly prepared for verbal confrontation.

Shouting and wildly gesticulating, behaving like men several waves short of high tide, they are ignored by the business traffic making the 15-minute drive into the centre of Brighton. But someone's watching over them. From the beach wall there's a shout of 'Magic!' and the men turn, walking over a 80ft camera-running track placed carefully out of reach of the incoming tide.

Robson Green and Stephen Tompkinson have pulled off another superb scene. Part of their reward is piping-hot coffee and you can almost see what they are saying spelled out in their breath as they sip it, switching the hot catering cups from hand to hand. Behind them the waves keep crashing in from the ocean.

Purvis and Purvis Master Builders are all at sea.

Trevor and Joe Purvis, their emotional and working lives in turmoil following their building adventures in London, are now plying their trade by the seaside. It is a long way from home, from Newcastle, in every sense.

These are brothers very much out of water. But being played by two actors sailing high. Robson Green and Stephen Tompkinson are 'grafters'. It is a sensational combination.

The advertising for the first Granada Television Production, in association with Coastal Productions,

---

'I respected Stephen Tompkinson and Robson Green as people and as actors and I felt that the idea had a basis of truth in it'
— *Grafters* creator Michael Chaplin

asked: 'If they weren't brothers, would they be friends?' The marketing material answered its own question, asserting: 'Blood is thicker than mortar.' But that proved hard to live up to for Trevor and Joe throughout the first series of *Grafters*, which brought the Geordie brothers face to face with the wealth, distrust and ruthless helter-skelter of upwardly mobile London. The culture and class clashes provided much of the drama and, from that, the humour.

They began that series as brothers in trouble and ended it sadder, wiser and arguably better men. Which is where we come in in *Grafters* 2, which sends these two cleverly crafted characters on a journey, where they are helped and hindered by friends, lovers and rivals, old and new. As well as building projects to test their skills. And nerve.

Trevor and Joe Purvis are now among the lexicon of classic television characters. They are a unique addition to dramatic pairings because they do not fit into any previous format; they don't even look like brothers. Joe, when not in his beachfront shorts, is tight jeans and streaked hair; Trevor is comfort and brown ale. The conflict between them drives their story and that of those around them.

The millions who have watched Robson Green and Stephen Tompkinson bring the brothers to such believable life – one family wanted to hire Purvis and Purvis to renovate their home – cannot imagine them being played by anyone else. Jonathan Curling, the producer of *Grafters* 2, is adamant about that: 'With Robson and Stephen in place everything works from them. If there's ever any doubt about how something is working they are platinum insurance.

'They can bring moments alive on camera. The two actors have created unforgettable television characters. We have used them to guide the whole series. They work – it's our job to make everything else work around them.'

Which is why an engaging crowd of production crew is surrounding Stephen Whittaker, the director

> **'This is a dramatic exploration of relationships. In the end we will truly know what Trevor and Joe are all about'**
> - *Grafters* executive producer Sandra Jobling

of the early episodes of *Grafters* 2. On location at Shoreham the sun has brightened but that wind still bites. No one seems overly concerned with the weather. What matters is getting that shot of Joe and Trevor on the beach just right. It is intense and important, as it moves the action in Brighton forward.

Camera trainee Harry Hardeep Dhami, delighted to be getting his first chance to work in mainstream television with such a prestigious series, is moving equipment deftly into place in readiness for director of photography James Aspinall. Nadia El-Saffar, who is in charge of the make-up department, moves across the beach to pancake some of the cold out of Robson's and Stephen's faces before the cameras roll again.

'They're lovely, no bother to work with at all,' she says with a big grin, adding: 'All the cast are turns to us. They're the tasty turns.'

What drew audiences to the first series of *Grafters* was the humanity of the stories. This was not the Ewings of *Dallas* or the Carringtons of *Dynasty* or a family from one of the more audacious soaps. Viewers could believe in the Purvises, even if they gasped at what they got up to. Especially that Joe; although in *Grafters* 2 there would be much evidence that Trevor was indeed from the same gene pool.

Stephen Whittaker, a bluff, affable get-things-done-man, who ducks and dives around every scene, picking up every point, was involved in some heavyweight drama productions before signing on to guide Joe and Trevor through some more adventures:

'I had seen the previous series and I thought it had real heart. It was about people, about characters; I thought it had its raw edges and that it wasn't slick in a way that a lot of other, similar series television has become. With television stars as the driving force

Co-stars, TV brothers, friends, Stephen Tompkinson and Robson Green on location with Brighton's Palace Pier as a backdrop.

what you end up with are simply star vehicles.

'I respected both Stephen Tompkinson and Robson Green as people and as actors and I felt that the idea had a basis of truth in it. It was not about the police or about hospitals. It was about people who just happened to be builders.

'It's about the human condition and human relationships. Within it, what you have is all the sibling rivalry and all the complexities and contradictions in a family, in relationships. It's about the loyalty of the brothers to each other through thick and thin against, you could say, the rest of the world. We're all going to experience in one way or another similar things from our own perspective and that's what makes it such a terrific series to work on.

'Everyone can bring something to the set because we all have a relative somewhere who gives us much happiness. Or, of course, nothing but problems. When you put the two together you have a solid foundation for building strong situations and that means good drama.'

When the first series of *Grafters* began, Purvis and Purvis were hired by yuppie couple Paul and Laura (Neil Stuke and Emily Joyce) to turn their new but ramshackle house into a dream home. Joe was something of a carpenter but Trevor Purvis was a novice DIY man. The Purvis brothers weren't cowboy builders – they were dude builders.

Sexually, Joe is a cowboy. That is apparent from the beginning of the series when we see him take off from Newcastle in the soon-to-be-beloved camper van, Irma, with his latest lover Janice (Eva Pope) on board. Janice is somewhat disenchanted about her naughty weekend in London when Joe stops to pick up Trevor. And Trevor's wife Karen (Tracey Wilkinson), and their baby Daniel (Clive and Luke Martin).

Superstar charisma – Robson Green is an expert at seducing the camera and proves it as Joe.

> ## STAR QUOTE
> *'I found it quite exhilarating'*
> – Neil Stuke, Paul in the first series, on hanging off the ladder over a 60ft drop

The road from Tyneside to London is noisy with bickering between Karen and Janice and when they finally arrive the two women immediately turn around and head home. Trevor and Joe, as they always will, have only themselves to rely on. And the kindness of strangers . . . like Paul and Laura.

Self-made man Paul is obsessed with proving to rich girl Laura that he is master of their future and the house is the foundation on which he wants to build their destiny. That being so, the house becomes the catalyst for all that will happen. And things begin with a bang – one not involving Joe. It is Trevor who nearly blows himself to bits trying to light the gas cooker in Paul and Laura's kitchen.

'Robson and Stephen are the heart of the series – they are a magnetic draw on the camera, on your attention'
– Grafters producer
Jonathan Curling

Disgraced, the brothers slope off back to Newcastle. It is there that we get some of the background to the Purvis family. Joe meets up with his former wife Mary (Mary Woodvine) and their daughter Josie (Leah Kindleyside), who he is clearly not comfortable with. It is also obvious that Trevor, honest and loyal, has not understood that his marriage is a sham; he is out searching for work to keep Purvis and Purvis – and also marital life – intact. Meanwhile, Joe is Jack the Lad. He is self-centredly seeking the good life in all the wrong places.

Despite a blazing row with his brother, Trevor smoothes the way for them to return to work for Paul and Laura. They end up making a speedy return. Joe is back in the arms of Janice when her policeman

11

husband Ray (James Gaddas) returns home. Luckily, Trevor is there to tell Joe they have been rehired for the London job and helps him escape. Off they race down the M1 with the cuckolded policeman in pursuit.

A storm has burst over London and Paul and Laura's home is being flooded after a roof tarpaulin has been torn free by the wind. Paul scales the scaffolding in an attempt to get the tarpaulin back in place. In subsequent action, the brothers get away from Ray and save Paul who is hanging on to the scaffolding for dear life . . .

'The Grafters' had begun their adventures – and millions of television viewers were hooked on the characters and storyline created by Robson Green's longtime friend Michael Chaplin.

It was a Geordie plot from the start.

Sandra Jobling, executive producer of *Grafters* is, like Robson Green, a director of Coastal Productions. She first met Robson in Newcastle when he was a young actor applying for his first-home mortgage. She recognized him as the porter Jimmy from *Casualty*. She helped him then and, drawing on her financial and legal background, has been doing so ever since. With Coastal, she has been involved with various programmes including *Touching Evil* and *Rhinoceros* and was delighted with the concept of *Grafters*.

It was about people and places she could completely understand: 'It was a project I felt I could usefully contribute to at all levels. When you have a good understanding of how the characters tick, it makes a creative contribution so much easier; it's impulsive and that way a higher percentage of ideas and thoughts for characters work. *Grafters* is always true to its roots and that is part of what has made it so popular with viewers. Audiences do know when you are not being honest with them and this series is always honest.'

The concept certainly appealed to Simon Lewis, controller of drama at Granada Television, and Susan Hogg, his deputy. It was not long before a night out in the West End of London with the lads from Newcastle would convince them to co-produce both series of *Grafters* with Coastal, and to be

STAR QUOTE

'Mum was a big influence on me. Teaching was a vocation for her so she's a great encourager'
– Stephen Tompkinson

executive producers on the series.

But, at first, things did not go according to plan for Michael Chaplin and Robson Green.

Superstar smile – Stephen Tompkinson who has stamped his authority and emotional warmth on Trevor.

CHAPTER ONE
IN THE BEGINNING

And the Lord said unto Cain,
Where is Abel thy brother?
And he said, I know not:
Am I my brother's keeper?
— Genesis 4:9

Michael Chaplin's ideas come to life in an upstairs room of his home in a quiet street in Putney, but when the pressures of domestic life intrude too much he will take off to faraway spots to concentrate on the words. Writing has always been part of his life. His late father Sid Chaplin is revered for his work especially in the north-east of England.

Michael is a veteran of prime-time television, having adapted the P.D. James novel *Original Sin* and written several episodes of *Dalziel and Pascoe* as well as other series. His first stage play was *In Blackberry Time* which he wrote in 1987. It was produced at the Live Theatre in Newcastle and starred an unknown actor called Robson Green.

There the seeds were planted for *Grafters* which would become such popular entertainment more than a decade later. Michael, a quiet, courteous man, recalled the genesis of the show which also reflects his own career and background: 'The project started because I have been pals with Robson for quite some time.'

After leaving university Chaplin became a journalist in Newcastle with the Thomson Press. He was a graduate trainee on the *Newcastle Journal* and was scheduled to move to *The Times* in London after his indentures. But *The Times* went off the street for a year and he went for a job in television at London Weekend where he worked as a researcher, producer and then finally an editor in the current affairs department.

'I started getting interested in fiction in the mid-1980s and that coincided with an opportunity that came up at London Weekend to develop an idea that I had. Then my dad died in 1986. He was a novelist, short-story writer and playwright based in Newcastle. The year after he died, a company called Live Theatre in Newcastle approached me and the celebrated playwright and television writer Alan Plater, who was a great friend of my father, to write a play based on his work.

'We did that together and *In Blackberry Time* was the first fictional piece that I wrote. It was about my

---

'He is quite an exceptional, natural actor'
— Michael Chaplin on friend Robson Green

dad's life and his concerns. He is a bit of an iconic fig-ure in the literary and cultural life of the north-east.'

In the cast of this play, in one of his first roles, was a lad called Robson Green, who was then about 20 years old. He had left school at 16 and become an apprentice in the shipyards. But he'd gone to a youth theatre in North Tyneside and been bitten by the act-ing bug.

'He was very successful at youth theatre, left his apprenticeship and became a full-time actor, which was quite a risky thing to do. Particularly from his kind of background. His family were all miners as indeed were mine.

'With *Blackberry Time* – and this was the first time I had seen him – it was quite clear how good he was. He was a mesmeric actor. He has this quite natural emotional pull across the screen or stage which makes you want to watch him; you're interested in what he's doing and what he's thinking and what he's feeling.

'He is quite an exceptional, natural actor really. That's not to say that he hasn't acquired technique along the way but he had something even then; something quite special. We got on.'

Soon after *In Blackberry Time* Robson's career took off, as he was given parts in a television play called *A Night on the Tyne* and then in the BBC series *Casualty*. Chaplin didn't lose touch with him, though, as they were both still involved in Live Theatre; also Chaplin's wife came from Newcastle so they both had family in the area.

'Robson and I have a mutual friend, Max Roberts, who is the artistic director of Live Theatre. He also ran the youth theatre that Robson had come up from and Max had been kind enough to give me my first writing job in theatre – both of us have maintained the friendship and collaboration. I've written five plays for Max over the years and we've just hung out as mates, gone to football matches.

'Robson has always been a very generous person. When Newcastle were in the UEFA Cup a couple of years ago, they were in the semi-final against

The Purvis Clan at grandad's funeral: Uncle Alan (Berwick Kaler), Trevor, Joe, Lennie (Maurice Roeves) and Aunt Maureen (Annie Tobin).

Master of the House: Neil Stukes as Paul outside his dream home.

'This shower room is not a problem . . .' as the builders said to their clients.

Monaco, so Robson rings up and says, "Would you like to come? I'm organizing this trip to Monaco." So I said, "That's really sweet of you but I was actually thinking of going anyway and taking my sons." But he said, "We'll all go." So Robson organized it all and we had a major row because he refused to let me pay for anything, including the two boys. It cost hundreds and hundreds of pounds. Anyway that tells you something about what kind of guy he is.'

Every time the two met they'd discuss how they should work together soon. Robson's ambition extended to developing his own material; he'd never be content just hanging around as an actor and waiting for roles. In 1996 Max Roberts approached

Chaplin with the idea of doing a play about football on Tyneside. This would eventually be produced as *The Beautiful Game* at the Theatre Royal in Newcastle.

'It was about the history of Newcastle United but it was also about this family, a father and son. That was very well received. Robson co-produced that through his company, Coastal Productions, with Live Theatre and the Theatre Royal. He was already acting as a producer. At the end of that he said: "Can't we do something with it? Can't we develop it in some way for television, maybe we can think of splitting it up?"

'I thought, and he agreed, that we could take to television a version essentially about a father and son who were Newcastle fanatics. They go off to support their team in Europe and instead of coming home after the match, they stay there and go to the next away match somewhere else on the continent.'

Robson and Chaplin took the idea to Simon Lewis and Susan Hogg who were then heads of drama at United Film and Television Productions. They had started *Touching Evil* with Robson, and Chaplin had worked with them on *Original Sin*. Everybody seemed to get on well so Robson suggested a meeting between the four. Chaplin recalls:

'A dinner was arranged at the Meridien Hotel in Piccadilly (a dinner which became infamous because of the ludicrous amount of money that we paid for a bottle of brandy). Fairly early on in the evening I pitched this football idea and they liked it but they thought that these two Geordies were going to be interacting with Italians and Germans and that never quite works on television. We'd already had the disastrous *Eldorado* soap about Brits in Europe, so there was not much enthusiasm.

'We hadn't yet got past the soup and there it was, our idea, lying in flames on the table. Robson asked me if I had any other ideas. I just started pitching this idea which had its origins some years before and always struck me as something that had a lot of potential.

'When I was a telly journalist, a current affairs person, a mate I worked with, at some point in the heady days of the 1980s when house prices were going through the roof, came into a bit of money from an inheritance. He bought a house in Notting Hill, which had become a very fashionable area long before the movies and Julia Roberts and Hugh Grant moved in.

'Prices were taking off even then and

because the housing market was crazy he could not get a builder to do it up. He really just wanted someone to decorate it from top to bottom. He could not get anyone anywhere and he was talking to a neighbour about it and they said, "Oh you want to get Harry and Joe. They've done quite a lot of jobs in this street."

'Harry and Joe turn out to be two Geordies who'd come down originally to do a job for a kind of ex-pat Geordie who happened to live in this new street. For a kick-off they were really good at what they did, they were reliable and they were much cheaper than any fly-by-night merchant. They just

> ### *'DIY? I'm still trying to crack housework'*
> — Emily Joyce who played Laura in the first series

Emily Joyce, as Laura, proving that those who DIY together stay together.

got loads of work; as they were painting, the next-door neighbour would come and say, "Ah, while you're here, do you think you could pop in and have a quick look at the job I need doing." They did job after job after job in the street, including my mate's house.

'What lodged in my mind was that they didn't waste money staying in a hotel, they lived in a van. I also think that, because I'm from Tyneside, I've always been interested in the contribution made by people who come from outside of London and keep it running. That was the beginning of *Grafters*. I know it's not very glamorous, not very Hollywood – my mate's house needing decorating. I was simply intrigued by the lives of these lads who had come

down south to make it; the reality of what their lives were about.

'Then, I thought about the whole difficulty of trying to maintain home life while they were away. Add to that the whole sort of class and culture thing. I imagined this street in Notting Hill with middle-class, upwardly mobile couples in publishing and media and the City. I could see dramatic potential in the contrast with these northern, jobbing, working-class lads.

'I was recounting all this at the Meridien Hotel, over the brandy. I don't know whether it was the good drink, or whatever, but they said: "That's really good. I think we could do something with that." Robson asked later: "Where did all that come from?" So then we all sort of staggered off into the night. That was the spring of 1997.'

Chaplin had various other projects on the go at the time but between jobs he began working up a treatment for the idea:

'Most important was the central relationship between the two men and obviously we did a lot of thinking and talking about that. Originally they were just a couple of mates but I then thought that if they were related, it would be stronger. They were going to be father and son and then we thought that was a bit of a cliché. How about if it were two brothers? That's what it became.

'I think the essence of drama is conflict so I thought it would be good if one of the brothers was a bit of a blag merchant, constantly biting off more than he could chew. His dreams ranged way, way beyond his capacity to realize them. And then the other would be just an ordinary kind of "Joe" who is fixated not on work or ambitions but on very simple family things. That's what motivates him.

'I thought that if they were living together, if they ended up together in a van, those differences would be constantly chafing between them. They would both be getting into trouble in their own lives partly as a

Dangerous liaisons: Eva Pope as Joe's could-be fatal attraction, Janice.

Janice trembles as her lover and policeman husband Ray (James Gaddas) discuss the merits of grievous bodily harm.

result of their own characters but partly also because of the contrasts and conflicts between them.

'If they were in Newcastle, they would have somewhere else to go. It's not the working time that's important, it's the time when they're sitting eating together, or they're trying to get to sleep or something else is going on. So the action needed to move out of the city – they had to be thrust together.

'Being fish out of water also means that quite often they have to stand together, which is another contradiction. A lot of the time they can be at each other's throats and saying "I've had enough of you"

and then something happens that means that they've got to shout: "He's my brother, you can't say that." They end up having to cover for each other, in work as well as personal stuff, and are constantly wrong-footing the other characters, themselves, and the audience.'

Simon Lewis and Susan Hogg recognized the potential and commissioned Michael Chaplin to write a first-draft script. Robson was a natural for the charming dreamer Joe, but the problem of who would play his brother exercised all those involved. As Michael Chaplin explains:

'The question of who was going to play Trevor was going to be a very important issue and we had a couple of meetings about it but I was at a football match with Robson and he said to me: "What do you

think about Stephen Tompkinson for Trevor?"

'I thought it was a really brilliant idea – and it was another example of Robson's generosity because Stephen is a heavy hitter. Some actors might have said, "Oh get somebody who's not terribly good, or not terribly famous", to make themselves the real star. Robson doesn't think like that. What mattered to him was getting the casting spot on.

'Sandra Jobling was already working with Robson on *Grafters* at this stage and so Stephen was sent a copy of the first script and a lunch was arranged in London at a very posh hotel in Park Lane. It was bizarre because it was the week that Diana was killed and there was a curiously unreal atmosphere at that time. I was early and I walked off the Mall and up through Hyde Park and past all these people. I had such a feeling of apprehension.

'We had this lunch and talked about how the character of Trevor would develop. I was getting ready to do my pitch to Stephen and his agent, Barry Brown, when somebody said to Stephen, "Well, what do you think?" And he said, "Great. I'd like to do it."

'That was it! I was entirely redundant. He didn't really want to know anything else. He had just come out of *Ballykissangel*. He was obviously looking for new things to do and he just bit on it straight away. What I think he liked in particular was that it's slightly unusual as a piece – which other people have said – that it's hard to pin down. Is it comedy? Is it drama?

'And that was always part of my vision for it: it would make you laugh and then it would make you cry and that would happen obviously in the same episode but sometimes it would happen in the same scene.

'Getting Stephen on board was a piece of inspired casting. I think he was intrigued by the creative challenge that Trevor presented. Joe regards Trevor as dead boring. It's actually in the dialogue: Joe says, "You are really dull." Sometimes, of course, he really is. But Trevor also has complete integrity. He has a way of behaving and being and he sticks to it through thick and thin. How do you make somebody who is notionally dull, interesting? I think that was the challenge Stephen picked up on.'

Granada, of course, was delighted at getting Robson Green and Stephen Tompkinson together in an original drama. Now Michael had to get on with the writing as well as plotting out what happened in the other episodes.

'A series as promising as *Grafters* has to be written yesterday. When they give the green light and say, "Can you have it ready for September please? We want eight parts", there is quite a lot of pressure in meeting that deadline.

'In an ideal world, I would have liked to have written it all but I simply didn't have time. If you've just got one guy writing everything it's going to take a long time. Now producers use two or three writers. It's partly because series have longer runs than they used to, which is an American thing; the Americans always used to say that six episodes is nothing.

'I wrote episodes one, two and four. Originally I was due to do episode eight but it just didn't pan out that way. I had the same director for all of mine – David Richards, who I had never worked with before but I thought was very good. I think he got a handle straight away on the characters and what it was about. It was a tricky thing to pull off.'

It was Richards who found the house which they would use for Paul and Laura's new home in need of renovation. Was this choice important to Chaplin?

'The house is another character. I was quite specific about what the house should look like and I thought it had to have a personality. Originally I'd set the series in Notting Hill but times have moved on in the area. The chances of finding a place there that had been run down for years and years until it was bought by this young couple who wanted to do it up – it wasn't credible any more.

'It had to be somewhere else, which is why we ended up in Blackheath. I went to that house, and the first time I saw it I thought, this is just perfect: that view of London out the back window, and the odd configuration of rooms, the size of the rooms, the height of the ceilings. It was perfect.'

The brothers' van, Irma, was another character. But why Irma?

'I don't know why or where it came from, I just thought it sounded slightly exotic. It's not like "Betty"

Trevor and Joe seek solace following their grandad's funeral. Newcastle will never be the same for them.

or "Elsie" or something like that. It was sexy in a way and mysterious.

'In fact the van is very much bigger than I'd imagined it. I was thinking of a sort of dormobile, something just a bit bigger than a normal van. When I first saw Irma it was a shock: it was as big as a house. There was a good practical reason for this, which was that anything smaller would not have accommodated the filming equipment. They had a massive amount of stuff to shoot in that van and in order to do this they needed something big.

'It was quite funny when Robson was called upon to drive that thing. He said it was dead scary. It was like driving a double-decker bus.'

As the plot unfolds the dilemmas and decisions faced by Trevor and Joe involve all those around them. Trevor's marriage falters and he is confused by the attentions of Laura. On the other hand, Joe has no doubts about why Laura is being nice to him. At the same time we see the pressures of working in the

The Lady of the House: Emily Joyce who received masses of fan mail for bringing Laura to life on screen.

'I thought the house had to have a personality'
– Michael Chaplin

City taking their toll on Laura's husband, Paul.

They are all caught up in the stress of modern living. It takes Joe and Trevor back to Newcastle to deal with family problems. It sends Laura back to her father for help and advice. And it drives Paul up the wall. And Laura into bed with Joe.

All the time the dream house – the symbol of all their undertakings – sits in the background. And it is there that all their contacts and conflicts are drawn. Until, finally, the only real conclusion is achieved.

'My last episode is the one where Trevor and Joe go back to Newcastle and their grandad dies,' explains Chaplin. 'There was a lot of discussion about it because it didn't contain a lot of caper stuff, unlike the other episodes. This episode was about an old man dying and the family facing up to the funeral and examining what was going wrong in their lives at that particular point. It had quite reflective dialogue, a heavy episode. There were some people involved who were saying things like, "Is this too sad? Is it too heavy? Does it lack incident and excitement?"

CHARACTER JOE PURVIS   ARTIST ROBSON GREEN

STORY DAY 5. EPISODE 7

CONTINUITY PHOTO

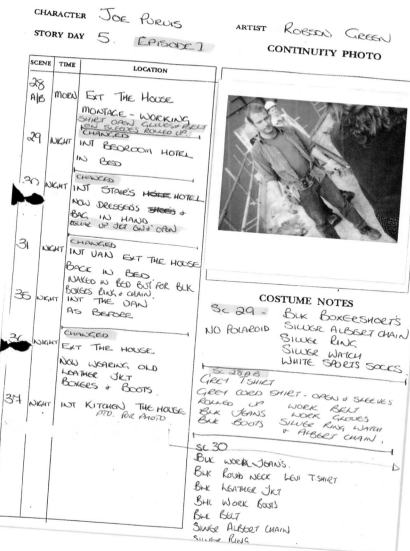

SCENE	TIME	LOCATION
28 A|B	MORN	EXT THE HOUSE
		MONTAGE - WORKING
		SHIRT OPEN GLOVES + BELT
		ON SLEEVES ROLLED UP
29	NIGHT	CHANGED
		INT BEDROOM HOTEL
		IN BED
30	NIGHT	CHANGED
		INT STAIR'S HOTEL HOTEL
		NOW DRESSED'S SHOES +
		BAG IN HAND
		COLLAR UP JKT GND OPEN
31	NIGHT	CHANGED
		INT VAN EXT THE HOUSE
		BACK IN BED
		NAKED IN BED BUT FOR BLK
		BOXERS RING & CHAIN
35	NIGHT	INT THE VAN
		AS BEFORE
36	NIGHT	CHANGED
		EXT THE HOUSE
		NOW WEARING OLD
		LEATHER JKT
		BOXERS & BOOTS
37	NIGHT	INT KITCHEN THE HOUSE
		PTO FOR PHOTO

COSTUME NOTES

SC 29 - BLK BOXERSHORTS
NO POLAROID   SILVER ALBERT CHAIN
SILVER RING
SILVER WATCH
WHITE SPORTS SOCKS

SC 28AB
GREY TSHIRT
GREY CORD SHIRT - OPEN & SLEEVES
ROLLED UP   WORK BELT
BLK JEANS   WORK GLOVES
BLK BOOTS   SILVER RING WATCH
   & ALBERT CHAIN.

SC 30
BLK WORK JEANS.
BLK ROUND NECK LEVI T.SHIRT
BLK LEATHER JKT
BLK WORK BOOTS
BLK BELT
SILVER ALBERT CHAIN
SILVER RING

enriched the writing of Trevor. Certainly in that funeral episode. I suddenly thought, well at the end in this episode he should find out that his marriage is over. There are no longer just suspicions, he's told it's finished. I thought how interesting it would be if Trevor – placid, calm Trevor – should suddenly flip and just go completely off it.

'I mentioned this idea to Stephen, and asked him if he thought it was right, and he said it was a really good idea. Then, of course, Trevor feels really bad and guilty about losing control.

'I wrote the scene where he just tears his wife to shreds, partly because she implies that she's leaving him because he's boring. He really lets rip. Then there's a touching scene later on where she brings his suit for the funeral to his dad's house. They are both feeling guilty and so it's a tender little scene. Both Stephen and Tracey Wilkinson said they loved doing that scene.

'Drama is always interesting when people are talking about one thing and thinking about another and that's clear to the audience because they understand that people do that. They try to convey something to each other but they're not talking about it. I mean, it would have been a less interesting scene there if she'd come and said, "Sorry", and he'd said, "Sorry". So instead he's saying, "Thanks for bringing my suit", and she says, "I've had it pressed", and, "How are things?" Of course, Stephen and Tracey are good actors. You can do wonderful things with good actors.

'It was interesting because my auntie just adored *Ballykissangel* and she was devastated when Stephen left. So when she heard he was going to be in this she was very pleased and I said, "Won't you be thinking of him as Father Damien?" She spoke to me after and

'They were all perfectly legitimate questions to ask but I think – and I think Robson and Stephen and the others closely involved felt – that at that point in the series the audience would have got so hooked into these characters that they would accept a change of pace. They're interested in these people, what they say, what they're doing, how they relate together. They want to know what makes them tick. Every episode doesn't then have to be plot-driven. I think audiences are very sophisticated; I think they can cope. The idea that they have to be fed something that is blandly predictable is nonsense.

'In the end the audience want to watch those two guys living their lives and all the things going on around them.

'I'm sure that the casting of Stephen hugely

a business level when the sexual tension is tangible and they are more and more drawn to each other. And Simon, having left girlfriends dangling in the north-east, may only be Joe's cousin but he's definitely from the roving-eye side of the family.

There will be plenty of opportunity on the street where they're working for everyone to get into some kind of trouble. And the Purvis brothers are always at the centre of it.

It was the dramatic strength of that sibling relationship which convinced Robson Green to bring his company, Coastal Productions, into the venture as co-producers with Granada:

'The great thing about the story is that the two main characters' values are so completely different. Joe's values are very materialistic and he becomes a womanizer, he becomes a guy who wants the big house and the flash car, and he thinks that will make him happy.

'He thinks he will get recognition by having a series of affairs in order to get what he considers "love". He is jealous of people who have love and jealous of people who have position and that's what he aspires to. Joe does terrible things. He leaves his wife and child – he does exactly what his parents did to him – but he becomes vulnerable when he's out of his depth.

'He's very different from other parts I've played. He's calm, controlled and he very rarely loses it. He chooses his moments very carefully. I'm sure a lot of people won't have liked some of the things he's done but hopefully they sympathize with him because of the strong relationship he has with his brother.

'Joe feels Trevor is an unnecessary financial burden on him and he is constantly looking over his shoulder to make sure his brother is in tow. He's completely upfront whereas Trevor just isn't.

'When we were younger I was very protective of my brother David who's three years younger. When I was seven and he was a little lad I made sure he was OK at school and for years we shared the same bedroom. He soon got physically bigger than me and

Bird's-eye view of the behind the scenes 'grafters'.

now I know he would look after me if ever I was in trouble. I always remember one particular fight when I realized I wasn't "big brother" any more.

'With Joe and Trevor it works the same way because the brothers spend time together – and have a history.

Where did the inspiration for Joe's look come from? He looks more out of place than just another northerner working in the south.

'The look for Joe came from a bloke I saw in Soho in London. He had the tinted hair, the tight jeans and seemed to be a throwback from the 1980s. I thought: "That's Joe, that's what he would wear." The guy was Joe.'

And Stephen Tompkinson is Trevor. No one asso-

Stephen Boxer as Geoff, a man who is apt to jump to wrong conclusions as series two unravels.

Camera! Moment of inspiration: searching for just the right angle.

ciated with *Grafters* would argue that anyone else could have become Trevor so completely. Stephen Tompkinson has worked hard to create an unforgettable character, and this is what he has to say about him:

'At first glance, Trevor might seem a little behind the times and not as up to speed as the rest of the world. But this is because, in a very quiet way, he is incredibly heroic; he's a man of great integrity which is very rare today.

'He sticks to his beliefs which are quite simple – he wants to support his wife and child and that is his complete raison d'être, whereas Joe has his eyes on much bigger things and is able to go much further in life on bravado and charm.

'Joe is able to improvise. Trevor is more likely to drown and that's why he relies on his elder brother to get him out of certain situations.

'Trevor is there to remind Joe of his roots and

keep his feet on the ground, enabling him to tell the difference between reality and fantasy. Trevor has walked away from his marriage rather than confuse his son Daniel. Karen, his wife, has a new man but Trevor still supplies financial support. That's how great his integrity is.

'I suppose the audience might feel sorry for Trevor but I think he's there to be admired. He's strong enough to stand on his own and not just be another statistic who cheats his way out of things.

'The central relationship is amazingly powerful. Joe and Trevor probably wouldn't have been friends if they were not brothers. I don't think that Trevor would be able to cope with Joe's lifestyle. But they do care about each other and it's because of the blood tie that they can't walk away from one another.

'Trevor knows that Joe needs him in the same way that he needs Joe. I know that personally; I've had a solid upbringing and so has Robson. My brother John is one of my biggest supporters and I love him very much.

'I love Trevor, too. I think a lot of people do.'

CHAPTER THREE
TEAM LEADER

'It always comes back to Joe and Trevor at the centre'

– Grafters 2 producer, Jonathan Curling

Jonathan Curling is a producer with a long list of credits in prime-time television drama. His television mini-series *Amongst Women* starring Tony Doyle was nominated for a BAFTA in 1998. He had been invited that year by Simon Lewis and Sue Hogg at Granada to consider working with them. He could develop his own material but, first, would he like to take a look at this show about two brothers from Newcastle, with a view to taking it over for a second series.

During a rare break in one of his regular 18-hour days, Curling talked about how Joe and Trevor Purvis became an intimate part of his life:

'At that point they were still shooting the first series and there was nothing to look at, so I read all the scripts and thought it sounded pretty interesting and then cuts came through for me to look at and I thought it looked really good.

'What really appealed to me was that it was contemporary, it was funny, it was touching, it was a very nice mixture of truthfulness and comedy. It was different. In terms of what television is putting out at the moment it was unusual and I'd not really worked with major television stars, so that was an added bonus. It would be a new experience under my belt.'

Budget-wise Jonathan had worked at two extremes: at the BBC he had worked on two big serials costing £1 million an hour each and then Carlton's *London Bridge* cost £100,000 an hour:

'*Grafters* was absolutely in the middle. On *London Bridge* we used to shoot four half-hour episodes, two hours, in eleven days. On *Grafters* we shoot two hours in 24 days so you've got double the shooting time which allows quality performance.

'The shift in British television since 1995 has been that talent, whether it's writers, directors or cast, have formed their own production company. They have more control over what they do, but also there's one way of getting an additional economical benefit out of it – they can control rights. Rights in television are worth money.

'Lynda La Plante, who created *Prime Suspect,* has

'Robson and Stephen transform something that might not be too clever into something magical' – Jonathan Curling

her own production company. Sam Burke who did *Liverpool One* did that through his own production company with Colin McKenna and there are a number of writers and one or two actors doing it. Robson Green was one of the first because he's got a very astute awareness of his own grounding and he doesn't want to get stuck in formal television. He's very strategic about what he chooses to develop and do. It's partly a creative thing that he runs his own production company and partly financial. You've got another string to your bow.

'Robson does have an input in *Grafters* because his company is an associate producer on the show. We have to respect Coastal's wishes and Sandra Jobling's as executive producer for Coastal. It is part of my job to talk to her every day and listen to what she has to say but in the end they would never abuse that relationship. They give myself and certainly Simon Lewis creative control of the show.

'What you learn working in soaps is that you respond to what's working and what's not working and you can write up or write down.

'The main thing, which I come back to again and again when constructing the story and storyline, is that we've paid a lot of money for two guys who are fantastically popular on screen. You would be silly not to make all of the story surround those two people even if you are going through other characters, in the end it's about their story.

'They are emotionally involved in it. If Joe is having a bad time with Viv then that will affect his mood and the way that he reacts to Trevor which will affect

EP: 5   SCENE: 63   DAY: 6

TREVOR
GREEN POLO SHIRT
WITH RACING GREEN TKS
BROWN BELT
BROWN BOOTS
WATCH
WEDDING RING.

JOE
WHITE V NECK T-SHIRT
BLK JEANS
BLK SQUARE BUCKLE BELT
BLK TRAINERS
SILVER ALBERT CHAIN RING
WATCH.

Just good friends. Trevor warms to Debbie (Luisa Bradshaw-White) after working on her flat in series one.

the way he reacts to Clare which affects the way she reacts to Nick which affects how he reacts to Joe which affects how he reacts to Viv: so in the end it always comes back to Joe and Trevor at the centre. That was the brilliance of the concept.

'Robson and Stephen and any other cast that you involve in the show will always make suggestions about their part, their character, the storyline and as far as I am concerned that is a resource that you should use. What they don't have and they cannot have is an open view of characters' developments episode by episode in the storyline.

STAR QUOTE

'I'd say I wanted to be a priest when Grandma was around because I knew I'd get my pocket money bumped up. I toyed with the idea when I was about ten. It was the most glamorous job I knew plus I had the guarantee of an audience every week'

— Stephen Tompkinson

'There is always a creative tension, a productive tension between what you are trying to do with your story and what the actors are suggesting that they bring to it. You have one story on the page; those actors will bring to it another dimension – and Robson and Stephen bring more to that than most other people do. They can transform something that might not be too clever into something magical.'

When Jonathan saw the way Robson and Lesley Vickerage as Joe and Viv worked together – 'the chemistry between them when were filming the first two parts' – he realized they had to rearrange the storyline:

'What they had created out of those scenes was a relationship which exceeded what was on paper. We changed the storyline to accommodate what we were seeing. You can never quite predict how what's in the script is going to translate into the end product.

'In a soap you're working that much further ahead in terms of story. If someone is not working well and I want to write them out it takes me 12 episodes in a soap. On *Grafters* if I'm seeing a great performance I can't change the scripts for the next block, but I can change them for the one after that. That's why the safe ground on this show is the scenes between Robson and Stephen because you know it works.

'I think that Robson has a particular range which he has played and he is always extending it. He is a man of action. He has an energy which is translated on screen. Stephen is absolutely the best in this sort of role because he has a soul which shows; he has a way about him, you believe him. You can see it on his face and he is a wonderful actor with his face. Just wonderful.

'What is really interesting is that even with two such totally different people – Stephen is taller, he's bigger, he's not neat physically in the way that Robson is – you can actually believe that they're brothers. You do believe this but as characters they are absolutely diametrical opposites.

'Families are interesting, and again this is why the series works because we've all had families and we've all had brothers and sisters. If you've got a stable domestic situation you've got no possibility of other relationships and in the end the series relies upon that possibility.'

As producer Jonathan was given a very free rein to create the story that he wanted and he was conscious of the need for something new:

'I felt after the first series that Trevor and Joe had done one house, they had been involved with one couple and they couldn't do that again. I had to do something different because otherwise we would have just been revisiting the same territory. That's why I decided to do something a little bit more complex.'

Jonathan had to assemble a creative team to begin work on the series, and first had to get the script and something to work with. He brought in Richard Stoneman who wrote one episode of the first series. He invited Judy Hirsh who came over from *EastEnders* as script editor and then Roxy Spencer who was the script executive at Granada. Curling had wanted to work with her since she'd script edited one of the four parts of *Falling for a Dancer* in Ireland. 'That was the core creative team and then we had Robson and Stephen and Darren Morfitt at the centre of it.

'The next person that I got on board was Charles Hubbard as line producer. With a project of this size it needed somebody incredibly sure-footed. Charles crunches the numbers and makes it work on an

But Trevor still has a soft spot for former wife Karen (Tracey Wilkinson).

Janice and Joe ask themselves, What's the point of this relationship? (previous page)

organizational level. Charles and I talk all the time, every day about every issue. We are going backwards and forwards all the time and he is a wonderful person to work with because he's very cool, which is exactly what you need. You know where you are and you can trust his judgement and what he organizes.

'When you're setting up a new serial, you want to lay very solid foundations and Stephen Whittaker was the perfect person for us. He is one of those directors who is incredibly good on character.

'There's an amazing number of people involved by the time you get to shooting: the basic crew for this is 55. And there's a lot of people you don't see. Those special effects guys are skilful because they've got to make it look good on camera. Although we make sure the actors are never in danger, every so often you do go into slightly unknown territory.

'I consider my role really as a communicator instead of a decision maker. And I was lucky enough to be able to get excellent people.'

From a storyline perspective, Jonathan found *Grafters* a refreshing change: '*Grafters* has got the best of both worlds. With *London's Burning* or any of those long-running series there are ongoing relationships. But first and foremost it's: "What's this week's episode about. What's the disaster? Where's the fire?" It's the same characters in a different situation every week. *Grafters* is a curious beast in that in some forms it is what I would call a serial – it's an ongoing story.

'You have a self-contained storyline every week. It has to stand on it's own but it also has to advance the overall story because it's about the major characters.

'Our premise at the beginning was to give Joe a

relationship which he had never had before, a proper loving relationship with a middle-class woman. Similarly, we had to get Trevor through a storyline which will involve him falling for someone else who isn't Karen his wife. Simultaneously we have to move them on in their relationship as brothers, because although they are brothers they are not the same at the end as they are at the beginning.

'The first time I met Stephen he said one of the first things I had to fundamentally understand about the Trevor character is that he's not simple, he's moral. He's got high morals. It's very easy with that character to take the piss out of him as simple and that's cheap. He's actually a man of integrity who's gone through a dramatic period in his life and he's coming through it.

'Very briefly in series one we saw Joe in love for half of one episode. Before it was "dream on, mate" so in the second series we were deliberately setting out a love affair which stretches across the episodes. And Robson – or, rather Joe – has to earn his sex; and the storyline has to earn it too. That's what is important in the business of drama: you have to believe that he wants to sleep with someone for whatever reason, whether it was a gratuitous shag or whether he's actually in love with them.

'When he went to bed with Laura in the first series we know, as the audience, that he's in love with this woman. As a character Joe is somebody who's not averse to having a shag when he wants a shag and that's how he treats women, but if you're trying to give him a different set of relationships, as we are in this series, then he's growing up. He's fallen for somebody and he's not in control in the way that he

> **STAR QUOTE**
>
> *'My Dad and I have been very strong together. He still creases me up. He and Mum still wind me up asking when I'm going to get a proper job'*
> – Stephen Tompkinson

Family ties. Aunt Maureen and Uncle Alan (Annie Tobin and Berwick Kaler) who keep the Purvis brothers tied to the north-east.

normally is. He finds himself in love.

'For a moment Laura was in love with him and I think that affected him and that's one of the things that we took into this series. That he had that experience and that he had been in love and he was dropped. It went wrong, so he's got that on his back and yet he finds himself attracted to a woman who is not of his class, not of his origins.

'Viv is a professional and at the beginning she is slightly patronizing towards him. Yet, she relishes his energy and his enthusiasm and against her better judgement finds herself falling for him and he, against all his macho instincts, finds himself falling in love with her and that's actually quite interesting.

'Viv is a key role and we saw an awful lot of people; every actress has a different quality and we were extremely lucky that Lesley wanted to do it. We wanted somebody who was an independent, contemporary and modern woman with her own identity; a strong female character. She seemed to have those qualities while also being warm and having the comedy to play when needed. Those were the elements we wanted and she had them all – and more.

'Katherine Wogan was also a prize. We saw a huge number of people for Clare Costello. The real problem for us in casting Trevor's love interest was that it had to be somebody you could believe Trevor falling for and who you believed would fall for Trevor: that's quite a tricky character to cast.

'We had constructed a *Romeo and Juliet* story. We looked at people who probably had more experience than Katherine and we looked at people who probably had more obvious sexuality.

'For me, Trevor would have run a mile from someone too sexual and she probably would have found him lovable but not fanciable. It was quite a difficult combination of characteristics we were looking for – somebody who is not too obviously beautiful, someone not too sexy, but who has sexuality and a very definite attractiveness. It's got to work together and Katherine just seemed to have all those qualities, being warm but slightly demure. She also had to be able to be up front and rough with her brothers.

'Lesley has got the experience of playing against Robson. But it's very difficult for Katherine to play against somebody of Stephen's stature who is a wonderful, wonderful actor – that both helps and intimidates. I take my hat off to her for going for it. It's not an easy part to play.

'We also had to construct family life on the street Purvis and Purvis move in on. We put Viv and Sam in with Lizzie who is a single teacher and Tom who is Asian and may or may not be gay. We then had Geoff and Pippa and their daughter Becky. All of that seemed to fall into place. But primarily we were trying to create a sensible household which was not suburban. We made it a singles household to give real breadth to the middle-class environment that Joe, Trevor and Simon come into. They have no experience of any of it.'

> **'We just thought Katherine would be perfect. She has an innate talent'**
> – agent Barry Burnett who gave Katherine Wogan her first big chance with *Aristocrats*

Jonathan Curling had to maintain the sense of the brothers being fish out of water while also introducing a new and fresh scenario. Where could they go that would provide as rich a vein of conflict and contrast as London?

'London-on-Sea, as Brighton is known, seemed to be the best place to go. It's a trendy town, probably the hippest town outside London. Added to which, it was nice to get away to an open environment and see the sea. Good chemistry.

'Also, on top of that, being in Brighton pushes the boundaries of Purvis and Purvis as a company; it takes them out of their league financially. You find yourself making these decisions without really making them. They just sort of happen.'

CHAPTER FOUR
THE FUN OF THE FAIR

'There's not an ounce of attitude about Robson'
– *Grafters* director Stephen Whittaker

Robson Green replaced those dinky beach shorts with a pair of Joe's tight jeans and happily wandered along the Palace Pier on Brighton's seafront. To accommodate filming the big dipper was not dipping and the barker at the concession stall where you could get three tries at winning a cuddly toy – Winnie the Pooh and Tigger the favourites – was remarkably able to restrain his vocal chords while the filming went on. But, a trouper, he mimed that any odd number did win a prize.

It was an important, delicate scene: Joe and Trevor were about to discover that their Uncle Alan might be friendlier with his personal assistant Melanie (Carli Norris) than even Joe might have dreamed. And that would give them a card to play in the ongoing game of chance with their most devious family member.

Crowds had gathered around the Palace Pier, the rather less revered cousin of the legendary West Pier next door. People pointed at Stephen Tompkinson patiently pacing the time away between scenes. Kids were sent off to cars to find the camera. Waitresses from the just-about-to-open pier cafés and restaurants made it well known that they would like an autograph.

Or a photograph with Stephen or Robson. Flash!

Bang! Wallop! What a picture!

Quietly understanding that they were disrupting the working day of the Palace Pier, the cast and crew of *Grafters* accommodated most of the fans' wishes, under the watchful eye of Jason Moyce – a man who looks as though he might worry Mike Tyson. And that's just verbally.

Jason runs Unit Security who have provided just that to the television and film industry for more than 20 years. Security and safety of the productions and all those involved are his concern. He will protect stars like Stephen Tompkinson and Robson Green from stalkers, the paparazzi and over-keen fans.

But Jason, who was amused to see George Cole's van from *Minder* being used as Nick Costello's transport in *Grafters,* was quick to point out: 'If we are on a public location like the pier we are happy to allow people to enjoy the filming because we know we are taking up a space.

'With stars like Stephen and Robson you know they will happily sign autographs and talk to people when they can. Our job is to stop someone who gets too enthusiastic. Our aim is to stop damage – not clear up after it.

'We liaise with police, local councils, parking authorities and, of course, residents. We want to

make filming as easy as possible and that means talking with street-cleaning services and that sort of thing. We can help in most ways but I've yet to sort out something with air traffic control to avoid aeroplane noise. You can have everything else in place and then there's always a plane buzzing over at the crucial moment.

'With a series like *Grafters* we are on location around London and Brighton so we map it all out in advance. If there are any areas we think might be a problem we advise the production. And when you are dealing with real professionals, as we are on this series, there is always a sensible compromise on risk, over what is worth doing to get something on film.'

Robson Green is always willing to make compromises but only if they dovetail with his determination to be involved in quality productions. He has his version of the Park Lane dinner with Michael Chaplin and the television executives.

'We had a couple of ideas to pitch at the meeting with Granada, one of which was this one although it wasn't called *Grafters* at that point. Then it was *The Van* but that was the title of Roddy Doyle's book and the film adapted from it.

'We were thinking about the two blokes in a van and suddenly over a brandy, before the others arrived, Michael Chaplin and I were concentrating on the title and came up with "Grafters". I knew Michael because I did *In Blackberry Time* and we were off on a good foot; Michael being a Geordie, a good writer – and a Newcastle United fan. Pretty solid credentials.

'One of the things that we wanted to do was to make something very north-eastern that had universal themes. An everyday life-story that these two human beings go through, emotional ranges that everybody in the world goes through, but it is set in the north-east.

'I thought that Michael would be the perfect choice as a writer and I was sitting there with him and he was saying what were we going to do about the relationship, because originally it wasn't about

Will they or won't they? Love amongst the emotional and building rubble.

two brothers, it was about the father and son from *The Beautiful Game*.

'*The Beautiful Game* was about the history of Newcastle United seen through the eyes of a family and centred around this father and son relationship. We wanted to investigate that and have them as builders working together.

'I talked with Michael over a few brandies and we thought, why don't we make them brothers. Soon Simon Lewis came in and we pitched the idea about two brothers who live in a constant state of misunderstanding. That was the pitch.

'We wanted it to be about two young men, as simple as that; building was the backdrop. We didn't want a complex narrative or plot, we wanted a basis from which two people talk about anything and you just want to listen to them. You are interested in what they say and in what they do because of the characterizations Michael created.

'The reaction to the first series proved we had all made it work. It was the most watched drama of 1998 and one critic wrote: "You are eavesdropping." He meant audiences were almost joining in Joe and Trevor's conversations and therefore their lives. The show never needed to hit anyone on the head. It was better, more subtle than that.

'The audiences were saying: "Oh are you doing that one about the brothers?" They were not going: "Are you doing that one about the builders?" That's the greatest compliment and it was a lovely feeling to have that reaction. We set out to achieve something and it is very rare for it to come off. It was a real endorsement and having Coastal Productions, my own company, involved was a wonderful bonus.

'Michael Chaplin can write really well about

family and that comes from his dad. It's all rooted in family and Michael can write the secrets, lies and the dreams and everything else we harbour as human beings, all within the family context.

'The only comparison the first series of *Grafters* received was with *Auf Wiedersehen, Pet*. I take that as an incredible compliment because I thought that was sensational. It was brilliantly written and the characters were really substantial and that is what they were saying about the characters in *Grafters*; they said that from the baby, from Daniel through to the grandfather, all the characters were wonderfully fleshed out.

'At the funeral, our dad had a fight with our Uncle Alan and there is something very comical about two blokes who are in their mid-fifties rolling around on

The serious side of drama as Trevor and Joe contemplate the future.

the floor watched by their sons.

'We sat around the coffin, the three of us. They held a camera on three characters and just let them talk. That is incredibly brave for TV today. Just let them speak and listen to the voices and I think that is why people were tuning in.

'Acting is really about doing something that you believe in. The one thing we say as actors is that you know your career's not going well if you suddenly appear on TV going, "Tasty, tasty, very, very tasty". The programmes I did initially, I had to do them for cash. I was broke.

'Acting can be an escape, an absolute escape from something that isn't too good and that is what I did. Suddenly I realized that there was an avenue there that I could explore. Max Roberts ran a youth theatre and I became involved. It was a great theatre and very well funded. He had a great set of students and we were working with professionals who had hands-

on experience. They had really done it. And that's why we listened to them. It was a lovely drama centre and I will never forget what it meant and how it helped people.'

Explaining why he set up Coastal Productions, Robson says, 'Back in *Soldier, Soldier* I knew I wanted to have more control and be able to develop independently and so I needed to know about the business side of it. From the start I wanted to be able to be more adventurous, to get back to the quality of *The Likely Lads* and *When the Boat Comes In*. All good writing. You just nurture what is there and help it along.

'And very early on with my company I wanted to be able to find a way to exercise the creative minds of young people. Give them that opportunity and then it's up to them.

'I realized how much companies get from advertising revenue. Advertisers want to put their adverts next to a programme that lots of people will watch and that's the basis of ITV. So the company is living off the ability of these actors. I always tell kids when I help them along to remember that agents and other people in this industry will live off your ability. Always remember that. It's a myth that an agent gets

Robson and Stephen with members of the Live Youth Theatre in Newcastle

you a job. They will have contacts but in the end it is your ability that gets you the job. Or lack of it that doesn't. There are standard agreements that agents are given and they pass them on to you. I don't have an agent. It's a wonderful position to be in to be able to choose.

'Every day I count my blessings. I was awful when I began in *Casualty*. I couldn't even walk and talk at the same time. I've still got that first episode – it's frightening. You can see my eyes wandering all over the place, not having a clue what I was doing. I can remember going home after each scene and thinking I would never work again. When I started in *Casualty*, I never dreamed of the money I'd be earning later. Or that I'd have been in a popular show like *Soldier, Soldier* and that people would be interested in what I was doing. I'm in a nice position; economic stability gives you options. That's what *Soldier, Soldier* gave me. I can choose the things that I want to do, and that's a very privileged position to be in.

'There was a total financial motive behind getting into music with Jerome and I've now hung up the microphone – but I enjoyed it while it lasted. We

realized we could make money quickly. All we had to do was stick with the pop star stuff for six months. You wouldn't believe what was going on. They wanted us to go to America and Japan. The market was huge – it was a madhouse. So we did what we had to and got out. If we had stayed there we wouldn't have been able to continue acting, and at that time it would have been the death of us.

'Jerome and I met a lawyer and talked about how much money we could make out of the music industry. *Soldier, Soldier* was being watched by 17.5 million people. We were popular characters. We could both sing – not brilliantly, I admit. We predicted that if we put out a record we could easily make £1 million each.

'I use my money productively. I invest in the arts in the north-east. I've put up bursaries for actors and I'm trying to give back something which the north gave me – an acting job and an Equity Card.

'*Grafters* has Coastal written all over it; the philosophy that all good drama stems from relationships and script and characterization, not from special effects. Hopefully Coastal will continue to push that forward.

'I am on the same wavelength as Michael Chaplin and it goes beyond going to football matches together. Michael and I think the same. We believe in the same sort of politics. We have very similar values. Very similar philosophies and similar aspirations and dreams.

'We believe in investing in people, giving people chances and choices. As a child there were times when I wanted to say "No" and I wasn't allowed. Of course there is right and wrong and you need to provide that guidance, but give them choices within their life.

'Investing in young people to give them the ability to create not only builds confidence but allows them

STAR QUOTE

'The only time I get out of control is when I watch football. I'm allowed 90 minutes of being a lunatic, usually I'm quite placid'
– Robson Green

to see the world; that's what drama did for me as a child. I was given this book called *Animal Farm* by George Orwell and I'm just: "This is incredible." Then, in this little youth theatre I went to see Macbeth.

'Michael Chaplin is very similar. If he sees something he will nurture it and he will invest in it. The school we have helped to set up in the north-east has got 300 students from an age range of seven to 25. We've got a film school with a five-year investment plan and three full-time teachers. We have bursaries and Michael does workshops and stuff. I mean, what a thing to have and be part of and help create. If you want to look back . . .

'I read an article in which Anthony Hopkins – and I think he was feeling a bit vulnerable – looked back on his life and it was like: "What a wasteland." I thought: "No, man. Look at what you've done and what you've created for others and what people have taken from you."'

On the possibilities of even greater fame and what he requires in the roles he chooses, Robson puts his cards on the table:

'I won't go over to Hollywood just because the received wisdom is "Well, that's the next progression." If LA send me a decent script that would be different, but I don't want to do something for the sake of just going over there. What we see over here from America is the polished end. We don't see the rubbish. If I was ruthlessly ambitious in terms of my career then I'd be in Hollywood now, but I'm not. I'm not saying I'll never go and do something there but I'm not moving right this minute.

'I think I might have trouble with the material there anyway because, for me, the most important part is getting the writing and the characterizations correct. *Reckless* was wonderful but I said it wasn't because of me. I may have been all right in it but the actual story was a stunner and Paul Abbot was responsible for that.

Joe comforts his brother who runs into serious trouble with the law as the action heats up in series two.

'I did research for *Casualty* and it was simple the tack that I was going to take. Porters, the ones I met, will avoid doing anything at any cost. The intriguing thing I realized is that they are the first who see the patients come in, they follow their journey out into the corridor, into surgery, into the wards, and they follow the patients through the day.

'They follow the whole character, which was never investigated. I suggested that Jimmy would follow a patient I'd seen coming in and we'd trace their journey; and whether they make it or not makes the drama. So there is this emotional involvement. You have to have that and audiences no longer expect perfect people.

'I think if Joe did have it all together it would be boring. That's the one thing. He wants security. Trevor is decent; in Joe's eyes he's boring. He needs to get a life but what's interesting about two people being in a state of misunderstanding, is seeing that they have separate values. Trevor is very straight-forward. His values are decent and honest and he is full of integrity. He would never harm any-one. I think that's what would be on his gravestone.

'Now Joe's values are com-pletely devoid of anything emotional. He's not in touch with his emotional self. He lives in denial which is com-plex in itself and which a character like that can stretch for eight episodes. His values are materialistic: big car, big house, girls, women but noth-ing precious in his life. He's had a kid, he's divorced; there's nothing precious there. With Trevor it is. If you put those two values together, we have the drama.

'They are two brothers who fight on equal terms. Even though Joe seems domineering, Trevor always wins as well in his own way. So in the end no one in the arguments really wins.

'Joe, especially because of his relationships, leaves behind him all this debris, which he doesn't deal with. Somebody said that Trevor or Simon should be behind him with a brush. It's an interesting image because that's what the guy does – drops emo-tional debris.

'He is macho man. He has to prove him-self to a woman and he has to sleep with her

because he needs to prove to her that he can perform so there's nothing emotional about that. It's just something mechanical. That's his way.

'Yet Trevor deals with it on an emotional level and that's the difference between the two. When something does get through to Joe, it's too late. It's always too late. There was a scene where his ex-wife says, "Joe you've never been loved, you don't know how to love". Then she ends it by saying, "I don't even think you know what love is." To which Joe replies "You meant that to hurt."

'I've seen lots of "Joes". The make-up, the "look" for Joe was intriguing. How he looks is important to Joe; it's an integral part of his character. He has to be immaculate.'

Robson is aided in his portrayal of Joe by excellent working relationships:

'We've had some great directors who have always known the character and you can always make things better and add to it. A lot of directors shout "Action" and they just expect you to do something and they'll accept it. On *Grafters* the directors have made enormous contributions.

'I struck gold with Stephen Tompkinson because I've never come across an actor like him, who is a wordsmith, who has an incredible memory for lines, and history and movies. His recall is so quick but his choice and his changes are always for the better, always to improve; and he is very giving. He never thinks about his own lines, he thinks about other people's. Steve works all the time and that's great for the rest of us.'

On how he draws on his own background to develop Joe, Robson says, 'No matter what anybody says, there is no place like home and that's what we miss when we are away. Trevor misses Daniel. Joe just misses his home, and it has always been the same with me. There is something about that place. I can't wait to get home, to touch base.

'Take the north-east accent. If it's in the right context, it is the most beautiful thing to listen to. I love listening to my dad speak. There's something incredibly romantic but real, not sentimental, about it. And if you give characters the right values and lines in a production, it's a joy to augment it with the right accent. I think we manage that but our characters' intelligence also comes out.

'We do set up some stereotypes but they are immediately broken down. We've tried to construct characters that confound these class expectations. The characters exist and you've seen these brothers before. I think the series has incredible integrity. I won't do another one.

'Whether Coastal will con-

Money talks in the building trade: Laura gets out the readies so construction can continue.

tinue with it is another matter. I think it's important that you leave something when it's on a high and, I know it's a cliché, but always leave them wanting more.

On the future, Robson explains: 'I am always looking for ideas, for stories. Especially with Coastal Productions as I hope we are all about strong projects and stories that say something and take us forward. We have one in the works which involves the mining village of Dudley.

'I learned the history from my father and grand-father who were very staunch socialist lads. The General Strike of 1926 lasted 10 days but the miners' strike lasted 26 weeks and what went on in that little village sparked the downfall of the General Strike.

'There was a derailment of the Flying Scotsman. Eight men were wrongly imprisoned for it. The story is about the wife of one of the eight men who fights for their release. Her husband spent eight years in jail but she finally proved that he and the other men could not have lifted the rail which made the train crash.

'I heard this story and went, Hang on: the fellas who were in prison lived just down from our house. The guy who cut my hair, Arthur, who is dead now, was in prison for eight years. I didn't know then – it was later when I found out when I read a book called *Stop the Wheels Turning* and another called *No Regrets* about the story.

'I have found video and documentary footage and met the villagers. This event split the village; it was a political set-up. Business and government had to stop the General Strike and these guys played patsy.

The big front-page headline was "Derailment of Flying Scotsman. Hundreds injured." There was one passenger with a sprained ankle.

'The most amazing thing was the truth. The train was carrying actors from Edinburgh and live lobsters and crabs and milk. All these locals, mostly miners on strike, rushed to help the passengers. The first thing that confronted them was all these lobsters marching towards them. It was just bizarre.

'It's also an incredible love story. That is the human contact with it, the narrative and plot, for essentially the woman just wants her fella back.

'Another thing was, the miners couldn't afford lawyers, they had to defend themselves in court and three of their friends turned King's Evidence. They had to cross-examine their friends in court knowing they had falsely betrayed them. These guys were worried for their lives. The police had told them that if they didn't say these things, other charges would be brought.

'There was one miner and he wasn't too bright – there was something a bit different about him. He was collecting grain growing around the railtrack for his budgies. He said he derailed the train and spent four years in prison. The propaganda was: "Make an example of them. Look at what the miners are doing. They are killing innocent people."

'And it worked – the strike ended.

'Also I'm learning fencing – or should be – for a show called *The Last Musketeer*. It's about a fencer who because of a criminal record can't make the Olympic team. He has a choice – either to turn back to crime or to train this Glasgow girls' public school fencing team for a European championship.

'It is an amazing sport. You have to be fit, seriously fit. I'm alright but I just did a thirty-second exercise and I was exhausted. It's so quick. I work out four times a week but the fencing I'm doing twice a week and then there will be an intense period of four weeks' training.

'It's important I think because this character is a fencing master. I've got to look like I can do the thing. I don't want the classic stuntman doing it and then

Irma stands proudly in the background as officialdom damps down Paul and Laura's grandiose housing plans.

the camera cuts close in and Robson pulls his mask off. I don't like doing that.

'After that I do this film *Blind Ambition* which is about an Olympic athlete who has a car accident and loses his sight. In order to keep his work he enters the para-Olympics and trains for them. It's about the relationship between him and his coach, his son and wife. It's this triangle that revolves around him. It's beautifully written.

'When I worked with Jerome Flynn on *Soldier, Soldier* there was an episode where Jerome was injured and lost his sight for an episode. He went and did the research so I'll nick what Jerome did. When you cut off your own sight you'll be listening to somebody but you don't focus on anything. Your other senses kick in and that's what happens to you when you're blind. You look through, look beyond.

'That's what you have to think all the time and there's a lovely scene at the end when he's on the track talking to his coach who can't keep up with him and he's going: "Don't lose it for me." It's just wonderful. It's that discipline of looking through, you know.'

Unlike Joe, Robson has achieved great success in his life. He ascribes it in part to his family:

'Upbringing. That's exactly what it is. Mum and Dad and Grandmother loved everybody. There was a lot of love there and it all helps. At school I was always interested in theatre but there were no courses. When I was nine, I played Joseph in *Joseph and His Amazing Technicolor Dreamcoat* but I really wanted to be Pharaoh because he had all the great songs. I pretended I was able to sing and dance. Boy, did I learn fast once we got on stage in front of all those people and I couldn't do either.

'My tutor was the careers officer and when I told him I wanted to be an actor he said: "You'd better forget that. You can't do it. You need experience of the acting profession in your family and you have none, so forget it."

'I haven't seen him since I left school but I really hope he watches telly.

'I was the kid who never got a girlfriend. I suppose I was an ugly kid with an awful haircut. My teeth weren't so good and my dress sense was well, let's just say ahead of its time. I'd go up to girls and ask

> ## STAR QUOTE
> *'I can't conquer live interviews on TV, so I'm not going to do them any more. I've done* TVam, Richard and Judy, *and each time it was terrible. I wanted to be political and interesting, but I came across as a gibbering idiot'*
> – Robson Green

them out and they'd turn me down flat.

'My parents were unhappy together and their impoverished circumstances certainly didn't help. The worst thing in the world you can have is debt. There were stages when, as a family, we thought the electricity was going to be cut off. Debt collectors were always coming round and we were constantly under threat from the bailiffs. It was a constant worry to my parents. What a terrible way to have to live your life and bring up four kids.

'Growing up in poverty hasn't made me more careful with money but it has made me enjoy it. I'm scared of being poor again but it won't happen. I understand what's at stake.

'Fame for some is a process of alienation. The more famous you get, the more important your roots become to you. That's why my home means so much. It's about belonging. But there is no point having fame and doing nothing with it. The best thing is that it puts you in a position to do things. That's why the school project is so important to me. There are kids out there just like I was who want to act and now I have the ability to help them.

'It is a ridiculous assumption that you can't still hold socialist beliefs and have lots of money. I don't associate socialism with poverty. If you've been poor and had nothing you embrace the things that money can bring you. I can use my earnings in a very productive way. By producing my own films and plays I am re-investing in people. I think that's very

We're a couple of swells. The stars of the show show their style for the camera.

important.

'My dad was a great singer, but he didn't have the drive to do it for a living and didn't have the choice of what to do, either. He had to go down the mines. When my mum watches me on television now she says she can see my dad, and I catch myself copying his mannerisms. If he'd had the chance, maybe he could have become the Montgomery Clift of Dudley.

'I'm not into all that luvvie stuff. I've never felt a part of it and never will. It's not real. I like the fact that I'm touchable. People come up and give me their opinion. I come from a small mining community where everyone knows everyone and everyone talks to everyone. At home people don't say: "It's Robson Green", they say: "It's Anne Green's laddie". It's like being part of a greater family. I never aspired to this kind of fame but I'm not one of these people who hide from life. I know what it's like to have nothing.

'I am so happy with my life. I have everything I ever wanted. I live a few miles from where I was born but my life is so different. I wouldn't be anything without this place, without family.

'That's the thing they're saying about *Grafters*: Stick with Joe and Trevor and you can't go wrong. As soon as you lose sight of Joe and Trevor, you've lost the lot. It's good stuff and Steve really enjoys it as well, he loves the scripts.

'I had great fun working with Steve again. He gave me a lovely present on the last day of the first series – Eric Morecambe's favourite tie. That's a good pressie. I gave him a picture of Stan Laurel, because if anyone should play him it should be Steve. His timing is superb and he's got the walk and everything.

'I've never seen spontaneous applause at a read-through like when we did *Grafters* with Stephen. I mean spontaneous. Everybody was packed in on the set and it is the finest piece of sight reading that I've ever seen. He gave the character 100 per cent. It was there, the very first episode.

'My copy was signed by Alan Shearer because he was mentioned in the first episode. I lean over and I say "How are you Grandad?" "Oh, you know, how's

the team doing?" and stuff like that. I say: "Don't worry, Shearer's still knocking them in." If your team are doing well, you feel good about yourself.

'And I do. I've done enough to fulfil an acting career. It's a job that I enjoy but it's not everything. When I go home I vacuum and I wash dishes and I walk the dog and I don't think about acting, and on Saturdays I go and watch football matches. That's what it's all about.'

CHAPTER FIVE
FLAMING HELL

'Stunts? I like my face.'
– Robson Green

Throughout his tour of *Soldier, Soldier*, Robson Green avoided doing his own stunts, explaining: 'The others are brave – and I'm not. There is a certain amount of danger that goes with a stunt and I like my face.'

But he broke his rule for an episode of *Touching Evil* when, as Detective Inspector Dave Creegan, he was set aflame and dumped in the ocean. Stunt co-ordinator Terry Forrestal persuaded him to do the scenes solo.

'I always said I'd never do stunts but Terry told me they would be controlled enough and safe to do. I had so many suits of clothes on I couldn't have been burned. I was put out by a fire-extinguisher.

'You can always tell the difference between the actor and the stunt double. There was a scene in *The Gambling Man* that I did when the house was on fire and I had to carry a body out. The stuntman did that and you just knew. When my family watched they shouted: "That's not you."

'That's why I was keen to learn to fence for *The Last Musketeer*, so that I would be seen in action. Not a double.'

Robson's *Grafters* double Martin Virgo and Stephen Tompkinson's lookalike Neil Morphew are on hand with the stars for a dramatic scene during filming of the second series. A quiet suburban area in Teddington, Middlesex, is itself doubling as the Brighton street of Viv and Lizzie, Pippa and Geoff.

To help continuity something suggesting the seaside or tourism – a boat in a front garden, extras parading in holiday clothes – has been put into the scenes shot away from Brighton. Production designer Tim Putnam can often be seen frisking scenes with his eyes to ensure there are no bloopers like a Heathrow Airport sign on what is meant to be King's Esplanade, Brighton.

But today the fire brigade are out in force along with special effects technicians. They are going to make a bonfire of a rubbish skip and put Pippa under threat when the fire spreads to her car. It is going to be a long day.

'Nothing will be done until all the safety measures have been tested and re-tested' – producer Jonathan Curling

---

'Nothing will be done until all the safety measures have been tested and re-tested,' says producer Jonathan Curling, keeping a watchful eye on proceedings at King Edward's Grove, Teddington, soon to be on the tourist maps as a *Grafters* location. The production company have hired a couple of homes but it seems all the residents are around to watch the fireworks.

Jason Moyce and his associates are monitoring traffic entering and leaving the street with the previously arranged help of the police.

Outside Viv's and Pippa's houses sits a large skip overflowing with debris. Tim Putnam inspects this carefully arranged chaos. Something does not look quite right. Stand-by painter Pat Roberts goes into action and that wood that looked too new to be burned suddenly has an older appearance. At the same time stand-by carpenter Glenn Paul Taylor is creating frameworks for the action.

Bob (Norman Gregory) stubs out his cigar in the skip while Viv (Lesley Vickerage) waits in the background. Stub that cigar one more time!!

William Parker as young Sam starts kicking a football around the front garden – it's not a game. He's rehearsing. Director Stephen Whittaker helps his young actor's nerves by showing his fancy footwork and heading the ball with William/ Sam.

Then, there's a call to action. Viv is seen leaving her front door and saying farewell to Sam for the day. She's off for a meeting with local planning committee member Bob (Norman Gregory). But before he joins her in the car, Bob throws his still-smouldering fat cigar stub into the skip.

Sam starts kicking his football off the garage wall and then, in a bit of a tantrum with his mother, he miskicks and the football bounces out towards the skip. He runs to retrieve it and sees the flames beginning to fan. He rushes to Pippa's house to tell her,

Lights! Camera! Flames! Special effects hot things up.

shouting: 'Mrs Marriot, Mrs Marriot!!'

Pippa sees the flames at the skip and near her car, an ageing two-door Citroen 2CV, snuggled up to and almost touching the burning skip. Shouting for her husband Geoff she finds her car keys and rushes to the car. She gets in, starts the motor and hits reverse – into the car parked behind her. In forward gear, she bangs into the skip and flaming debris falls on to the canvas sunroof which catches fire. Pippa panics and starts screaming.

Shocked, her husband Geoff can only watch his wife sitting in the blazing vehicle.

Joe, Trevor and Simon are walking down the street when they hear the shouts for help.

Behind the scenes the FX-team and camera crew are working quietly together; the camera is fire-proofed and as close to the action as possible. Firefighters stand behind the camera in case

anything should go wrong.

One moment the skip is a pile of rubbish not worth a glance – the next an inferno. Pippa's car is on fire. She's screaming inside it. Joe, Trevor and Simon are pounding down the street. Joe grabs a brick from the blazing skip, smashes the front passenger window and reaches through the flames to try and open the door. Trevor and Simon are trying to stop the car being eaten up by the burning debris falling all over it. Joe gets the door open and grabs Pippa just as the blazing sunroof falls in.

Joe shields Pippa with his body and slides her from the car. Trevor is covering Joe with his jacket, putting out the flames threatening his brother.

On screen it will be moments. To get it on camera was a long, hard day's work.

Harry Hardeep Dhami sets the clapboard for plenty of ACTION!

'In a series like *Grafters* where you have a great deal of story there is a need for action but it has to be credible. This is something that could easily happen – a careless moment and then, almost tragedy,' said Jonathan Curling. 'It takes a lot of planning and you are always aware of the safety of everyone involved.'

One of the major planners involved in every scene is location manager Kevin Holden. He has to find filming locations in Brighton and also around the production's home base of Shepperton Studios in Middlesex:

'The main concerns are always logistics and costs

but we have got to look to the script and attempt to feed it as well as we can. For *Grafters* I sat down with the designer and the director and we talked through it. We tried to establish between us a style, a feel for the locations that were required. You hope you're all on the same wavelength.

'Then I started to look at a number of considerations. The script and style – but also the practicalities of it. One then finds something which meets that combination of requirements. Sometimes you actually come upon interesting locations which then inspire you a little bit; perhaps to look at something in a completely different way. The logistical element is often as simple as, can you actually get near it?

'When Tim Putnam, the designer, and I talked

Marian McLoughlin as Pippa is rescued from her blazing car by Joe.

about the look of the programme with Stephen Whittaker, we thought it would be an interesting challenge. The series is Brighton based but you don't always want to be seeing Brighton Pier.

'We created Nick Costello's building yard here in Brighton but you can only justify doing it here if you have something around you which says: "We're down at the coast". This particular location has an interesting view out of the windows, and out in the yard, with the sea and the ships. It gives a different feel from Brighton seafront.

'That's not necessarily exactly what was in the script but of course we're looking to hopefully add something visually to the writing.

'Brighton sees quite a lot of filming and the council and the police are very friendly. There are difficulties in filming a seaside resort. It tends to be busy, particularly when the sun shines, and so there

He ain't heavy: Trevor desperately fights to stop Joe being burned to death.

are some problems with that but on the whole it adds to the production. We work with everyone – life cannot stop because of filming.

'We wanted to film on the Palace Pier and we arranged that we would be there up to lunchtime when the Pier becomes very busy and they want to start running the rides, operating the concessions. These are noisy and problematic for us and so we fit in what we want to do without causing too much mayhem.

'This has been a particularly good production to work on because there is a real team effort to get everything just right. We're all aiming at quality in every aspect of *Grafters*.

'I have to make judgements. Even if the location looks great, if I don't think that I've got a reasonable chance of making it work, I wouldn't offer it up as a possibility. It's much more difficult where you have a producer or a director who has seen something or has a particular place in mind which you then have to try and make work; sometimes you simply can't. If that means that the crew are all unhappy because

Pippa runs screaming for safety as Joe continues to battle the flames.

they are having to walk 300 yards to the set, then that's all part of the cost and there's a cost in time wasted by trudging backwards and forwards. It may not be desirable but, occasionally, you may not have the choice.

'When I first came into the industry I did some work on commercials. I remember one car commercial where we shot just five seconds a day over six days. We ended up on the M25 before it was opened, because we had a garage scene to build but they

Firemen and safety experts were close to the action throughout filming.

wanted the car accelerating out of the garage and an ordinary garage wasn't big enough.

'We built the garage on a part of the M25 and sat there with the entire crew from seven o'clock in the morning. It was a gloriously sunny day but we didn't want it sunny. We wanted it cloudy so we sat there all day long and did nothing and shot it in 15 minutes at dusk, which approximates cloud. On the commercial they had the luxury of doing that sort of thing but on a series we don't.

'Normally we would have weather-covered scenes. So, for example, when we were on the pier, the weather-covered scene was the interior of a pub

Grafters II - Episode 2, amended shooting script   23/04/99

88

55. EXT. STREET OUTSIDE PIPPA'S HOUSE. DAY.   15.52

PIPPA gets to the door of her car and starts to unlock it. The fire in the skip is increasing in intensity, with flames licking up the piles of rubbish and furniture. PIPPA gets into her car, gets it started and slams it into reverse. There's hardly any room behind her, however, and she rams the car that's parked there before she's had a chance to turn the steering wheel. Going forward again, she accidentally slams into the skip, knocking some burning debris from the top of a pile. The burning debris lands on the cloth sunroof of the car. PIPPA screams as the debris falls over the driver's door and causes the sunroof to catch fire. PIPPA panics and just sits inside the car screaming.

Within seconds, JOE, TREVOR and SIMON are there. Grabbing a brick from the burning skip, JOE uses it to smash the passenger-side window. Despite the flames, he reaches in through the broken window and tries to unlock the passenger door. TREVOR and SIMON, meanwhile, are pulling burning debris off the roof of the car. TREVOR shouts to PIPPA:

TREVOR
We're going to get you out.

GEOFF comes out of his house and sees his wife in her burning car. He just stands there, unable to move or say anything.

JOE manages to open the passenger door and he leans in to grab PIPPA. Just at that moment, the burning sunroof falls into the car. JOE pulls PIPPA underneath his body as he slides her out, shielding her from the blazing material with his shoulders and arms. In a second, they're both out of the car. TREVOR immediately covers JOE with his jacket and extinguishes the flames from the bits of sunroof that have stuck to JOE's back. JOE is in pain but his only thoughts are for PIPPA, who's lying, crying, on the ground.

JOE
You okay, pet?

PIPPA can't speak. She's still crying.

A RESIDENT comes along with a small fire extinguisher and starts putting out the flames in and around the car. Other RESIDENTS start arriving, watching all this from a safe distance, including LIZZIE**

SIMON takes out his mobile phone.

SIMON
I'll get the fire brigade.

GRANADA TELEVISION
in association with Coastal Productions

GRAFTERS II

EPISODE TWO
by
Richard Stoneman

SHOOTING SCRIPT

23rd April 1999
Amended Version

ognizing that one may have to give way to the schedule.

'We've not really got any studio-time in this series at all. It's all on location. We did do a day in the studio shooting around Irma the van. There's usually a pile of this stuff to do and of course we're trying to be ahead, working ahead of every-body else.

'In an ideal world, when one turns up on the day, once you've got everything set-tled there should be almost nothing to do. If you've got nothing to do all day then you've done it right first time. Although in the end there is always something.

'Also, on location, to a large extent we're kind of a PR. We're the public face of the production. Most of the places where we go and film the only contact that the locals will have with the production is via us, so there's always some sorting and PR to be done on the day, but hopefully not too much if it's been prepared properly.'

Part of Kevin's brief is making sure Brighton looks like Brighton, even when it's not. 'Audiences have expectations of what a seaside town should look like and so if it's Brighton it has to meet those expecta-

where Trevor and Clare met for a drink. We wanted to do it outside on the patio but we could have done it inside if forced to. And from the pub windows the cameras would be looking out over the sea. Even inside it would say Brighton.'

This job sounds like a compromise between the ideal location and the realities of filming. But Kevin prefers to see it rather differently: 'I think it's actually trying to get the best out of everywhere that you're going and get the best out of every aspect of the script – but at the same time being realistic and rec-

Grafters 2 director and soccer fan Stephen Whittaker puts the head in for William Parker who plays Sam.

tions or they don't believe you.

'This kind of architecture here is very recognizable. The architecture further back from the sea is from a very particular period and style and we can actually use that. It's a Regency style which is really when this town flourished. It was probably a terribly smart place to be along the Esplanade. You have larger tracts, towards the west end of Brighton and into Hove, of Edwardian housing which is meant to be where Viv and Pippa's street is.

'Then of course as you go back off the front you get into the smaller anonymous streets. I mean we've not really had to duplicate that but in fact we did use a restaurant in Twickenham. It had much of that kind of feel about it.

'Most people will believe it and if we say we're in Brighton then people will generally accept it unless you make a pig's ear of it.'

The length of time it takes to make a location move – at least an hour – means Kevin has to be sure there won't be any hold-ups, or shooting will be severely disrupted. 'The important thing is to make sure that you have covered everything. You learn not to rely too heavily on other people; you need to know what you're after is going to happen and not be subject to somebody turning up late, for instance.

'The first thing I did for a scene which was to be filmed in a flat at 5 a.m. was to see the people we rented it from and get a key. They were going to be in the flat overnight, but I'd be very uncomfortable just relying on somebody on the fifth floor to actually wake up when you press the bell.

'So I made sure I had a key to get in if they didn't wake up. That way at least I could get inside, get the camera gear in and bang on the door on the way out.

'This job has to be hands on.'

CHAPTER SIX
ANOTHER FINE MESS

'Without the words, we'd all be Marcel Marceau'
– Stephen Tompkinson

Don't think of them as 'Robson and Stephen'. Although they have established themselves as one of the great unconventional double-acts of dramatic television, Robson Green and Stephen Tompkinson are very much their own men. They like each other, admire each other. But they're happy to make their own moves and separate futures.

Robson would like Stephen to play Stan Laurel but will leave Oliver Hardy to another actor with more girth.

Stephen Tompkinson has established himself as one of the nation's most popular stars with television series like *Drop the Dead Donkey* and the hugely popular *Ballykissangel* under his belt.

At the movies, *Brassed Off* remains the thinking person's *Full Monty*, a hugely truthful and moving production which gave Stephen the opportunity to deliver some heart-wrenching moments.

He is quiet and serious, a little shy, it seems, of his achievements. He explained his aims, choices and why he decided to become Trevor Purvis:

'The choices I make are initially based on writing, that's where it all comes from and I can't kid myself it's any other way. I'm always conscious of wanting to do something completely different from the last thing – I fear being pigeon-holed. So, after *Bally*, I

needed something else.

'I've known Robson on and off for nearly ten years because we used to go after the same jobs, the current score being 2–1 to him. He did a BBC play called *A Night on the Tyne* and I did one on ITV called *A Nightingale Sang*. We were both up for Jimmy the porter in *Casualty*.

'My reward for coming second was a guest death in the first episode – so we finally got to meet and struck up this friendship immediately.

'He's a very affable man. We're very similar in many ways, so we constantly kept in touch throughout that time. When I learnt that this series was going to be happening and that I could be playing Robson's brother, I thought it was definitely going to be

71

Imprisoned man: Trevor finds himself behind bars having been set-up by Clare Costello's brother, Nick.

something good.

'I know his work and that I like him as a person and as an actor and I thought we'd spark off each other very well. We've never had a cross word. When I got to see Michael's script I thought it was lovely because immediately you are involved in the journey. There was no ploddy setting up and it was just straight in and it was terrific. I agreed to take the part without any hesitation.

'I gleaned from the script as well that the main relationship that needed conveying, around which everything else would work, was that of the two brothers. Knowing Rob as well as I did, I thought: "Great, we don't have to work on that". I knew that the makings of a successful project were there.

'When we began the director was David Richards who I hadn't worked for before. He had a beautiful air about him, a very calm man and very observant and gave us both a lot of rope to find the characters as soon as we started.

'We had a ball. It was a very happy shoot. It's cer-

Family man: Trevor on the beach with Karen and son.

tainly the most heroic character that I've ever played. I remember David Richards asked me had I seen *The Bloke's Story*, the story of this bus driver trying to keep his son away from more interesting Mafia ventures and being quietly heroic.

'I think in these benighted times Trevor does seem slightly out of kilter with the rest of the world and that can be misconceived as him being slow and a bit stupid. He isn't at all. He's just honourable. It's just so rare that you get to see someone like that. It's what makes him unique. I have great respect for Trevor, It's refreshing in a modern context because you don't see many characters like that.

'The brothers also have the father figure who could drop in to encourage them to think for themselves but also to look after one another; and they do need each other. Trevor does also get spiritual guidance.

'Me being six foot two and walking around with the baby was a beautiful device and the kids that we had were exceptional and stole a lot of the scenes. I

73

CHARACTER TREVOR PURVIS   ARTIST STEPHEN TOMPKINSON

STORY DAY I EPISODE 4

CONTINUITY PHOTO

SCENE	TIME	LOCATION
1	AFT	EXT TYNE BRIDGE. JKT OFF & OVER KNEE
2	AFT	INT VAN TYNE BRIDGE JKT OFF & OVER KNEE
3	AFT	EXT TYNE BRIDGE
4	AFT	INT VAN CITY CENTRE
5	AFT	INT HOSPITAL CORRIDOR
6	AFT	ALF'S WARD HOSPITAL JKT ON & OPEN COLLAR UP TOP BUTTON OPEN
7	AFT	ALF'S WARD HOSPITAL
8	AFT	INT CORRIDOR HOSPITAL JKT ON COLLAR UP TOP BUTTON OPEN
—		
14	EVEN	EXT TREVOR'S HSE AS BELOW
15	EVEN	INT TREVOR'S HSE JKT ON & OPEN TOP BUTTON OPEN
	EVEN	INT CORRIDOR HOSPITAL JKT ON & OPEN COLLAR UP
21	EVEN	INT WAITING AREA HOSPITAL

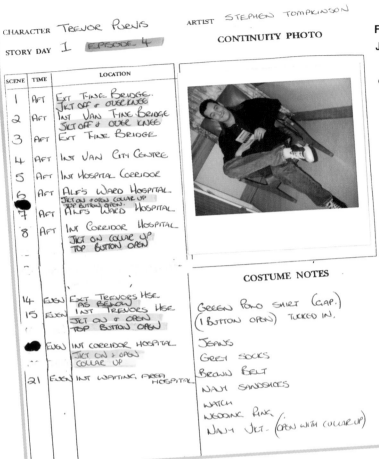

COSTUME NOTES

GREEN POLO SHIRT (GAP) (1 BUTTON OPEN) TUCKED IN.

JEANS

GREY SOCKS

BROWN BELT

NAVY SANDSHOES

WATCH

WEDDING RING

NAVY JKT - (OPEN WITH COLLAR UP)

Father Trevor holding baby Daniel with Uncle Joe.

choices he's made as well: having been in *Casualty* and then *Soldier, Soldier*, to be brave and reinvent himself as he did with *Reckless*. Forming Coastal Productions as well and the Live Theatre in Newcastle. He's putting stuff back in as well.

'Variety is the spice of life for me, so being able to do *Brassed Off* and then going back to the theatre in 1998 last year, and still doing *Drop the Dead Donkey* kept me buzzing.

'With *Grafters* we have laughs but the comedy isn't too broad because it is two brothers who have known each other all their lives. They have routines. They know each other too well.'

Stephen didn't have to try too hard to get into character for the building scenes: 'There would even be more comedy if I tried to do the building work. I haven't a clue – just not a DIY person. I can manage to pick up the phone and make someone else do the work. There was an awful lot of: "Here's one we prepared earlier!" during filming of the first series, which was fine for the character of Trevor who's meant to be out of his depth to begin with. But he applies himself wholeheartedly to his involvement. I'm sure there will be a lot of proper builders who wonder what the hell we are doing.

'But the important thing was to stay emotionally true to Trevor.'

Stephen had to liaise with Karen McKinlay-Gunn, the costume designer, in order to work out a look for Trevor. And it seems the cap fits there too: 'I said, well it was probably his missus Karen who would have done the shopping for him and I don't think he's fashion conscious at all. She came back with a load

think Trevor would prefer, if he was going to lose the baby, to completely walk away for fear of the kid getting confused with two dads and he would just let him have his life. However much it hurt him, he would make a sacrifice which would be seen as ridiculous and selfish from some people but it makes integrity his password.

'I'm a huge fan of Stan Laurel and always have been and I liked that sort of innocence that could come through with Trevor and allow me to have great fun with him but not make him look stupid. I didn't think he was a stupid man anyway.

'I love comedy but I'm too petrified to do stand-up. Stan was 37 when he started to do films and I'm 33 now but I'm a bit tall for him. Maybe if we get Robbie Coltrane to do Ollie there'd be a similar height difference. It'd be great.

'Robson encourages you to do different projects. He likes to try different things. You look at the

(Overleaf) The flame still flickers: Karen visits Trevor in prison and gives him some emotional help.

Trevor wraps himself around son Daniel, the focus of his life.

of stuff and it felt great when it was on.

'In the second series I'm having a romance with Clare. We don't know how it ends up, but we're having a great time. It's very easy because she's seen Trevor's uniqueness. He stands out from the crowd somehow and then when she gets to talk to him she realizes that he's not like other men at all, which is a very refreshing change because she has this elder brother who is a perfect match for Joe.

'And because she's in the business as well, he's probably used her in a way to make deals more attractive for people to come into his company. She can see through all that and so it's a revelation for her to meet somebody who's actually an honest man.

'Trevor has only slept with the one woman, his wife, and then in the first series there was someone else who was very attracted to him but he didn't feel ready. It's like a year on and I think he is ready. He finds things in common with her because of similar experiences with her brother, so they have an empathy immediately. It's all very family driven.

'I would imagine that Trevor will fall, and fall very heavily for Clare, which might be too much, too soon. He is an all-or-nothing type of guy. It's black and white.

'There's ambition there for me and drive and I do my best to serve the programme to the best of my ability. I'm much more of a team player than a prima donna. My first job was joining the radio rep and that was 54 players so the scripts were everything because you just have your brain and your voice to get over the author's work.

'It is very special because you are doing it for an individual audi-ence: they listen to what you're doing and they have to fit in the rest of the mental jigsaw – where it is set and what the character looks like and no two people are going to get the same vision, so it's really special. It makes you appreciate writers because without them we are speechless.

'It's much easier when 70 per cent of your work is already there on the page and then you're trusted to interpret the project. I wouldn't see any point and I wouldn't get any enjoyment in playing a lead in something that didn't tickle my fancy.'

For instance, Stephen was offered a lot of money to do a second series of *Minder*. But his agent Barry Brown pointed him towards something else that was coming up: a play at the Royal Exchange in Manchester – a four-hander with Richard Wilson directing. 'Barry said: "There's no money in it at all and you could have *Minder* for all this amount of money and a seven-month contract." He said if you want to do *Minder* I want you to come to the office

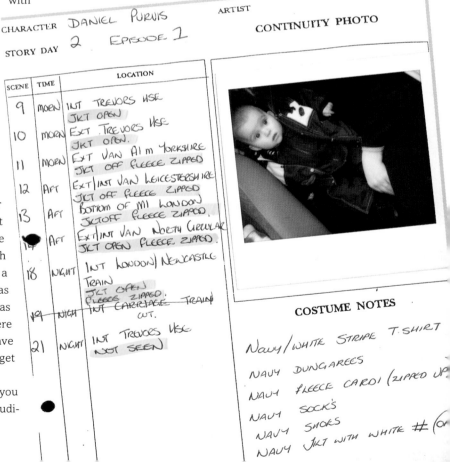

and look me in the eye and say: "That's the last job
we do for the money." He said: "I can't guarantee that
you'll be able to make up that money but I will guarantee you seven months' work."

'I adored the play and it was nice to have Barry
doing himself out of commission. It's lovely to have
that honesty and that backing; someone who is
actually looking after your interests rather than
their own bank account. I never had to sign a
contract or anything with Barry, he just said:
"The deal is this: I'll make you famous, you
make me rich." That's how agents should be I
think. That's a great foundation along with great
support from the family as well.

'And you need that foundation to build your
own confidence and hopefully provoke it in others
about you. I did feel ready for the responsibility
bigger parts put on you by the time I got them.
I've done a lot of solid support work in *Chancer,
Minder, The Manageress* and all those series I'd
done before. I might not have got a great deal of
acclaim, but I was learning and growing in confidence. With my face better known, I felt ready
for that leap. And along came *Ballykissangel* and
then *Grafters*. They are family shows and that
matters to me.'

Like Robson, Stephen draws on his north-
eastern roots and his strong family life: 'A lot of it
is for my family. I never want to do anything that I
don't think Mam and Dad would like or appreciate. I wouldn't want them to be embarrassed.
They're not prudish in any way but I wouldn't want
them to think that I was gratuitous, so that's an element that I base things on as well. We're not saving
lives every day, we're entertaining people.

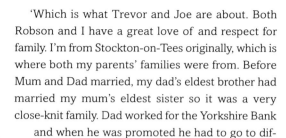

'Which is what Trevor and Joe are about. Both Robson and I have a great love of and respect for family. I'm from Stockton-on-Tees originally, which is where both my parents' families were from. Before Mum and Dad married, my dad's eldest brother had married my mum's eldest sister so it was a very close-knit family. Dad worked for the Yorkshire Bank and when he was promoted he had to go to different branches so we went from Stockton-on-Tees to Scarborough and then we ended up at St Annes, next door to Blackpool.

'Mum was a teacher and there was me and my elder brother John. They were amazing, encouraging me and I think that the older I get the more I'm appreciating what a wonderful stable upbringing I had.

'It was Grandad on Mum's side who, when all the grandkids were sat around watching Laurel and Hardy and all the slapstick, said to me, "Watch Stan", who to me, at that age, seemed to do nothing and that was the point. Grandad was very much like that, very dry humour.

'My brother John is a wonderful mimic, much better than me, and a real inspiration to me as well. Funnily enough he never had the same confidence as me to get on stage and do it. He works in a retirement home in St Annes-on-Sea. They absolutely adore him there.

'The line in *Grafters* about "If they weren't brothers, would they be friends?" is not a question for us. He's always with me; John and I are very good friends. I knew he'd like *Grafters* and my mum and dad get very involved in it because they like the brother thing very much. I get home three or four times a year and otherwise Mum and Dad will come to wherever I'm filming, so we've got closer over the years. We've never really drifted away.

Shower? No, we'd rather take a bath, thank you.

'Mum was a big influence on me. Teaching was a vocation for her so she's a great encourager. She's a junior school teacher so she's teaching ten-year-olds everything at the moment and she taught me to love literature and writing. That's carried through.

'My dad and me have been very strong together. He still creases me up. I can understand why families fall apart, it's inevitable sometimes, but I've been lucky in that respect. It's also someone to entertain and I can repay them all the trust that they invested in me. They still wind me up asking when am I going to get a proper job.'

But the die had been cast during that happy childhood: 'I came to realize as a kid that I wanted that escapism, and it's nice to keep carrying the torch. I was much more interested in cricket at first, and I sort of played with the idea of being a priest as well because that was sort of glamorous.

'But then there were teachers who were prepared to stay behind after school and put to use that energy and imagination that kids have by involving you in these plays and showing a whole alternate world to you as schoolboys. I was taken up with that straight away really, so I think at 14 it was getting stronger and stronger, this urge to follow it through.'

Stephen went to drama school in 1987 and the biggest period of unemployment he's had since was three and a half weeks when he went to Melbourne and Sydney to watch two Test matches. 'I have always had work, be it radio plays or voice-overs. I've been lucky in that I have a good ear for accents and if someone has written one sentence with five words in it there's five different ways to put an emphasis on it. You can talk about process of elimination and knock out the ones that will not give the right response to the next person. So technically, I've enjoyed radio the most.

'I enjoy *Grafters* too and it is a great help working with Rob. He comes to me for things and I go to him for stuff and I never get bored of his company at all. It's not like I've been working with him all day, so give me a break. Not at all. We have great fun and I like socializing quite a lot, but Rob's not the biggest drinker in the world and he does work in a different way to me. He doesn't consider himself a very quick learner so he really has to spend an awful lot of time

Marian McLouglin who brings energy and dignity to her portrayal of Pippa.

with the scripts, more than I do. I can look at something and "bang" it's in there.

'The crew are fantastic, it's lovely that they're laughing at the rehearsals because they're as much an audience as the eventual audience. The fascinating thing for me about comedy is that there are thousands and thousands of different ways to do a gag and some will work in some areas of the country as opposed to others. So you can't be rigid about this by saying, "I'm convinced it's going to be this way." Especially when you have a director saying, "Yeah, but just try it this way." There's a lot of give and take and you come to joint decisions.'

When Stephen received an offer to front one of the *Great Railway Journeys* series, he saw it as a way

people that are going to work together, so they're like a family for the next 20 weeks.

'If they respect each other, when you get into problems – because you always get into some problems, weather, light, not enough time, too many scenes to shoot – they'll work through it together. I think they are already doing that.

'That's always been important to me. I've worked with James Aspinall, the director of photography, two or three times and he's wonderful. He's 120 per cent. He's a clever, creative guy and very generous, but he stands his ground when he wants something. Tim Putnam, the designer, lives up in Newcastle and I've worked with him a couple of times before. He's brilliant but he's there to do a job – not pushing himself forward.

'It's about a lot of laughter and about making the right choices. Obviously, with Robson and Stephen as the stars you have a rather good start.

'Stephen and Robson work well together and whatever their own politics are, they seem to be working well and are very generous with each other. And they do work. There is a sort of healthy competition, but I've not had one wanting to outdo the other because they are playing such different roles. They've been very generous with me too.

'The camera loves Robson. I mean that in the right way. In my opinion, having now worked with

him for the first time, if he had the right vehicle I think he could be quite a big film star. He could be a romantic film star in the right way.

'He has a great understanding of the camera. Not knowing the camera can be a handicap to people. If you're worrying about the camera then you're worrying about all the other things. If you instinctively deal with the camera, as Robson does, you can find the centre of the scene.

'One of the things that Robson said very early on was that this project is very organic, and I believe things should be organic. I can come up on this set

| CHARACTER | ALF |
| STORY DAY | 7 EPISODE 1 |

ARTIST

CONTINUITY PHOTO

SCENE	TIME	LOCATION
63	MORN	INT HOSPITAL (IN BED IN HOSPITAL)

COSTUME NOTES

GREY PJ's WITH BURGUNDY STRIPE.
WHITE VEST.
HOSPITAL TAG.

Lennie (Maurice Roeves) puts Uncle Alan (Berwick Kaler) on the carpet.

every day saying, "do that, do that". If I did, I think I would be losing and so would the series. I never impose. I'll give them parameters and I don't just mean Robson and Stephen: any actor needs to work within a parameter and find things and experiment. As director, you might throw out a lot but it makes actors think rather than coming on and just performing.

'Stephen, I think, is a very fine actor, in a completely different way to Robson so they compliment each other. I think Robson is much more instinctive and he has great heart. Stephen also has heart and instinct but he has a great timing for wit and he's very quick with lines and situations. I mean, he would make a great stand-up comedian. He's very clever.

'I don't know how many more series they will want to do but I think they can go on and make lots more.'

THE CRITICS

The critics were bowled over by the first series of *Grafters*.

THE CRITICS

Daily Telegraph:
'Captivating comedy drama, excellent lead characters, Robert Lockhart's theme music works a treat'

THE CRITICS

London Evening Standard:
'A charming, loveable Geordie drama'

THE CRITICS

London EveningStandard:
'Proving to be ITV's best hard-hat drama since Auf Wiedersehen, Pet'

THE CRITICS

The Sun:
'Grafters just gets better – ITV's thoughtful and unpredictable drama'

CHAPTER EIGHT
SIMON SAYS

*'Darren as Simon has become more and more part of the series.
He's family'*

– Sandra Jobling

Darren Morfitt is smack in the middle of all the *Grafters* action. As Simon, cousin of Trevor and Joe, he is treated more like a younger brother. They boss him about. On and off screen.

Darren, a skilful footballer, starred as wonderboy player Dean Hockwell in Sky TV's *Dream Team* series. His TV brother was played by Daymon Britton. When word went out that the role of Simon was available on *Grafters* the two young actors both went for the job.

Darren was convinced his friend would get the role. He had connections: Daymon Britton's uncle is Robson Green.

But nepotism did not overrule casting considerations. 'We'd both heard of this thing called *Grafters* that Robson was going to do and that there was a part for Simon, apparently lasting only two or three episodes. We both went up for it,' says Darren.

'I presumed Daymon, as Robson's nephew, was going to get it. I think in the end he was just wrong for the part. So I got it, but unfortunately I was under

> **'They told me that they liked what I did and had decided to offer me more episodes – which I was obviously well chuffed about'**
> – Darren Morfitt

contract at Sky. They wouldn't let me go no matter what I said. I told them that I really wanted to do this job. I said I'd looked at the contract and there was a little clause that allowed me to get off. Eventually they must have looked at the contract too because they said I could go.'

Overjoyed at being free to go for *Grafters*, Darren attended a read-through in front of the producers: 'They told me that they liked what I did and had decided to offer me more episodes – which I was obviously well chuffed about.

'At the beginning I didn't think about being in the series for the younger audience. I was just trying to play a character from what I had been given in the script. I formed the character as somebody who looked up to Joe and had a close family history with the Purvis brothers. Robson and Stephen and I have talked about history and where exactly I fit in their family scheme of things and that's what comes across on screen, I think.

'Simon's mother and Joe and Trevor's mother, who has passed away, were sisters and Simon's

father is being a bit of a wally and he's long since out of the picture. Simon has basically grown up fatherless. His mother, because she's the closest thing to their mother, is important to Joe and Trevor and that is why they look after Simon. And, in turn, Simon looks on his two older cousins as father figures.

'I wasn't intimidated by the job. I was looking forward to it a lot because I feel very confident in what I do. But then, on the first day of the shoot I did get really nervous, and I was thinking, "Jesus Christ, I'm stood next to Robson here. This is really weird. It's him off the telly."

'Instead of taking me under their wing and saying, "It's OK, it's OK", Stephen and Robson decided they would completely take the piss out of me. Whenever I fluffed a line, instead of being nice, they would jump on me and say, "He's useless. Sack him." I quite enjoyed that kind of reaction. I learned a lot from them.'

When Darren started shooting the first series, he was 24 and Simon was supposed to be 19: 'It is funny how on set and in between takes and over lunchtime, it's difficult for them to react to me as an older and more serious person than Simon. They do know I am, really, but it's easy for me to just come out with

Darren Morfitt, who plays Simon, offers some youth attitude.

things that are more like Simon. It takes a while, a good hour after work, to get back into your serious self and have to think about things.

'Simon's very laid-back, and I'm not. I'm damn wary about things. I get depressed. Obviously, there is an element of me which can be dafter and flicker about and have a good laugh, but it's the tip of the iceberg.

'At the same time, I don't pin all my life aspirations on acting. I'm very serious about the scripts and I do the work at home before I come on set, but then I'll make light of it with, "It's only acting". I keep it all in

CHARACTER Simon

STORY DAY 4 . EPISODE 2

ARTIST

CONTINUITY PHOTO

SCENE	TIME	LOCATION
7X	MORN	INT HOUSE (IN BED) ∿ POLAROID
73	MORN	CHANGED EXT HOUSE (NOW DRESSED)
74	MORN	INT HSE AS POLAROID.

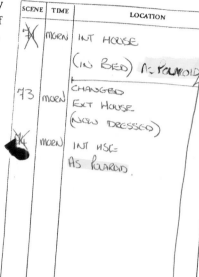

Sc 71

COSTUME NOTES

BURGUNDY T. SHIRT (WORN OUT)
GREEN COMBAT TRS
CAP + GLOVES IN TRS POCKETS.
BLK BOOTS.
RED & BLUE # SHIRT (TIED AROUND MIDDLE)
GOLD SLEEPER
BLK SILVER NECKLACE.

Sc 71 - NEWCASTLE UNITED TOP
BOXER SHORTS - NOT SEEN.
GOLD SLEEPER.

38

Grafters II - Episode 2, amended shooting script   23/04/99

25. EXT. STREET. EVENING.   20.42

JOE and TREVOR are walking towards the pub.

>   TREVOR
> You sure it wasn't your fault? Maybe you did
> get the dates wrong?

>   JOE
> No, no, you're mixing us up. I'm the one who gets
> things right. You're the one who doesn't.

They walk in silence for a moment. TREVOR's a bit pissed off.

>   TREVOR
> I'm surprised Viv's not coming to the pub.
> You're never apart these days.

>   JOE
> She's still working.

>   TREVOR
> So you did ask her?

Before JOE can reply, SIMON comes running up behind them, panting.

>   SIMON
>   (to Joe)
> Give us some money, will you?

>   JOE
> What for?

>   SIMON
> I might want to go out later.

>   JOE
> You're going out now.

>   SIMON
> But I can't buy you a drink.

>   JOE
> You never do.

'We used more and more of Darren as Simon in the second series,'
— said executive producer Sandra Jobling

explosions. It was naturalistic and it was very simple and very true, and that's the kind of material I hope to do later.'

Darren too believes that one's background can be important in the creative process: 'I think it helps that we share northern backgrounds. When I look at Robson and Stephen I know what they are thinking. We all know how each other's characters would respond to things. So it's very instinctive.

'It's nice to see Joe having tendencies towards more serious relationships. It materializes towards the end of the second series that he's starting to grow up – not that he's given up flirting. I'd be happy to see a more serious side to Simon too. Not in a big way, just a little hint. Things happen to you to make you grow up. For instance, how would he react to a girlfriend pretending to be pregnant? He's been shit on by his dad so he wouldn't want to do the same thing to someone else. He'd want to do the right thing, even if he didn't love the girl.

'Robson is very technical in his acting, and when I first started shooting series one I was impressed by Steve and his approach and what he was doing. He was very inventive. He's always got a trick up his sleeve. He would make something out of nothing, and I like that. I thought he was going to steal the show from Robson. And then I saw a rough cut of episode one and said, "Look at Robson. He knows what he's doing, man. He really knows his stuff here."

perspective. If it all stops tomorrow then I'll see it as having been a good laugh and that I've made a bit of money and that's that.'

Darren started acting at nightschool, at home in Hartlepool, when he was about 20: 'The first time I stepped on stage, it was just a mass of boards, but I got something I'd never felt before. It was a wonderful feeling. Obviously I had always been into films as a kid. The one thing that really got me when I was young was *Kes*. You don't have to have big

'I think it works really well between the two of them. Stephen does something which is character-based and Robson does little things when he knows what lens is on and exactly where the camera is and how it looks better; they are two completely different ways of working.

'I'm somewhere in between, I guess. I'm just trying to learn from everybody. I'm trying to learn from the crew. I'm trying to learn from Stephen, Robson and also the people who have little parts who come in. I'm trying to soak it all up while I have the opportunity.'

In between series Darren kept himself busy with *The Murder of Stephen Lawrence* – 'which was good for me to get my teeth into' – and then a series for the BBC called *Warriors*, which is about the first UN peacekeepers to go and sort out Bosnia and involved shooting in the Czech Republic for two months: 'It's about two lads from Liverpool who joined the army together and go over to Bosnia and it's all about how it affects them – what they see over there, compared to what they thought they'd see. It was quite harrowing and it did affect me. I feel more comfortable doing serious stuff than I do doing comedy.

'Instead of taking me under their wing, Stephen and Robson decided they would complely take the piss out of me. I quite enjoyed that kind of reaction. I learned a lot from them'
– Darren Morfitt

'But at the end of it all I couldn't wait to get back to *Grafters* and chill out and have a laugh for a couple of months.

'The comedy in *Grafters* works because it isn't just on the surface. There is more searching going on

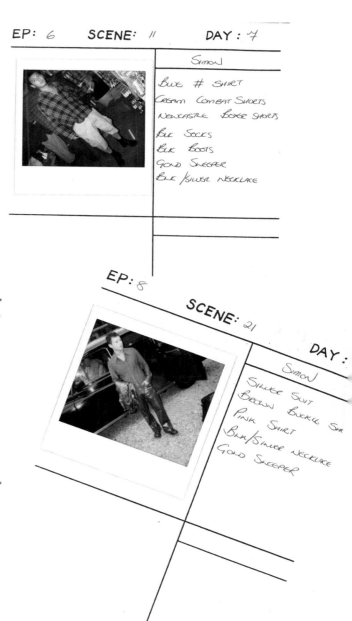

EP: 6   SCENE: 11   DAY: 7

Simon
BLUE # SHIRT
CREAM COMBAT SHORTS
NEWCASTLE BOXER SHORTS
BLK SOCKS
BLK BOOTS
GOLD SLEEPER
BLK/SILVER NECKLACE

EP: 8   SCENE: 21   DAY:

Simon
SILVER SUIT
BROWN BUCKLE SR
PINK SHIRT
BLK/SILVER NECKLACE
GOLD SLEEPER

Grafters United, but where is Alan Shearer when you need him? (previous page)

underneath. If you play the truth of a scene and play it for real and think about how you would really react, instead of just trying to achieve a laugh, then the humour will come out.

'There's also the question of how far you can really go. It's a fine line. Personally, I thought episode four dropped a little with all the funeral stuff – but for other people it was the best episode.

'*Grafters* is a brilliant opportunity for me. I'm not

> **'On the first day I did get really nervous. I'm stood next to Robson here. It's him off the telly'**
> – Darren Morfitt

some sort of fly boy who wants to make a pop record and be on *Top of the Pops* – that's not really what I'm about. I'm not after the limelight, I just want to do good drama. If the scripts are good then I'll do them for free, and if they're poor then I won't do them for lots of money – but there is always a little compromise that you have to make.'

Again the importance of family life outside, as well as within, the programme, is revealed: 'I just come from a very ordinary working-class background. We're a very close family and I have a girlfriend, Helen – we've been together for four years and everything is cool there. My sister has moved to America now, she works for the *Washington Post*. My mum and dad are over the moon. They just wanted us to be happy, which we are, and so they're happy.

'Obviously they get a little buzz about *Grafters*. They're my biggest fans. I don't want to blow this opportunity. If I've got people's attention then I want to be seen in the right sort of way.'

Relative disorders – can we please, play ball? A between-takes invitation to football action from Darren Morfitt to his acting mentors Robson Green and Stephen Tompkinson.

CHAPTER NINE
ROMANCE

'O Romeo Romeo! Wherefore art thou Romeo?'
— Romeo and Juliet (II.ii)

Trevor Purvis may appear an unlikely Romeo but Katherine Wogan is cognizant of the deceptiveness of appearances. And relationships. And dealing with difficult families.

She was seen in the summer of 1999 in the costume extravaganza *Aristocrats*, which told the true story of the Lennox sisters, who were born into one of the grandest eighteenth-century families. Adapted from Stella Tillyard's book it stretched corset elastic through the Georgian to the Victorian era.

She played the bitchy, snobby gossip, the Duchess of Richmond, who got her kicks from others' misfortunes. The Lennox sisters were embroiled in many mishaps, involving Royal scandal, sexual escapades, political intrigue and generational difficulties.

After that *Grafters* must have seemed like a pleasure cruise. It was a year after *Aristocrats* was filmed in Ireland that Katherine got the call-up for *Grafters*. As the daughter of Terry Wogan she is acutely aware of the rollercoaster world of show business.

She had been brought into a 1999 episode of

Dalziel and Pascoe by casting director Kate Day, who had the same duties on the second series of *Grafters*: 'I got called in to meet Stephen Whittaker first and then the process of formal auditions took place, and I got it. I couldn't believe it. I didn't think I had a hope in hell when I went for the first interview because I thought they'd go for someone a lot more established than me.

'For me it was such a fantastic job. It was a huge break. And so here I am as Clare Costello. It is a whole new and very fantastic world. I'm with the

'I was excited about the role and particularly working with such an illustrious cast' *— Katherine Wogan*

Doing time: Trevor hears jailhouse tales and doesn't like them.

With the building trade as a backdrop many of the technical crew on *Grafters* found themselves being enlisted to help on camera. For instance, stand-by painter Pat Roberts' hands stand in for Robson Green's or Stephen Tompkinson's in some work scenes.

Glenn Paul Taylor, the stand-by carpenter, was always available for advice or DIY: 'There was a kitchen scene and Robson made out he was putting a handmade kitchen together. I was putting the things together, and taking it apart, to make it looked as if he had actually done it. So each scene had a little bit more added. There's a little bit of gashed timber in the workmate and he's banging it and making it look as if it's a real technical piece of work for the actual kitchen.

'The scenes change. One minute the kitchen is unfinished and you can see plaster and then the next hour you'll go off and do something and then they want the kitchen finished. The nice part of it is that outside of the TV industry both Pat and myself worked on houses, so we could build you a house. I don't think Robson and Stephen could – but they're good at their jobs and we do ours.

'Directors are not very handy men. They wouldn't know how to plane a bit of wood. We do the action shot but it's a close-up on our hands only. It's on for two seconds. There was one instance with Paul in the first series wanting plastering on the house. The director said could you get them standing on the steps with a two-inch brush painting the wall. Now I said that you wouldn't do that. You wouldn't paint a large area with a brush; it would have looked stupid.'

EPILOGUE
END OF THE PIER

'Grafters is about relationships being established and seeing if they survive'
– Lesley Vickerage

Both series of *Grafters* have been about survival, overcoming circumstances, mistakes, jealousies, prejudices and all the other hurdles that confuse and conflict everyone's lives.

The engine that has driven the programmes has been the need to look out for one another; if we don't then lives do fall apart. What everyone with an interest, from professional critics to the producers, agree on is that the storylines are a reflection – often in a

'I think it is intriguing to wonder where they will go from here'
– producer Jonathan Curling

necessarily dramatic way – of everyday life. Fans have written in saying that something similar to what happened to Joe or Trevor had happened to them. There have, of course, been a raft of building tales – not all of them horror stories. And with the help of experts like stand-by carpenter Glenn Paul Taylor

Purvis, Purvis and Purvis: the firm of Trevor, Simon and Joe on location in Brighton. (previous page)

the screen DIY stars always looked as though they knew what they were doing. Robson and Stephen say that was the best part of their acting.

Stupidity certainly never entered into the filming of the second series of *Grafters* and, as the summer of 1999 drizzled to a close, the cast and crew were back in Brighton where the future of Joe and Trevor and their satellite relationships was being contrived.

All involved had witnessed the brothers' relationship develop on screen as Robson and Stephen became more and more familiar with their characters and themselves. 'It was natural progress,' reported Jonathan Curling, adding, 'but you have to put into that equation their great talent. As filming went on they brought more than we could ever have

123

imagined to the characters.

'They made Joe and Trevor progress, mature and, indeed, become different people. Interestingly, as that was happening the cast and crew warmed more and more to the series. I have been involved with plenty of television projects but I have never known such camaraderie. I think that comes with everyone being such professionals and knowing that *Grafters* is a quality piece of work. And with everyone pulling together everything has gone smoothly. Happily, all the drama has been on screen.

'With the storyline we have taken the boys on to a place where the future is open to them for any furthur Purvis and Purvis enterprises. Robson and

---

'There are difficulties filming in a seaside resort. It tends to be busy, especially when the sun shines, but on the whole it adds to the production'
– location manager Kevin Holden

Stephen have created a couple of memorable characters and I have always known this. They, as I always say, are where the great strength is. They draw the action and your attention to them.

'By the end of this series they have grown up and I think it is intriguing to wonder where they will go from here. At heart they are still Geordie lads – but Geordies who have now seen a little more of the country, witnessed different kinds of lifestyles.'

By now, familiar figures on the Brighton seafront, the cast and crew of *Grafters* had been almost adopted by the coastal resort. Filming there has given the series that particular stamp of authenticity that only location work can do. Although there are Brighton 'doubles' at and around Shepperton Studios, the on-the-spot camera work captured a special 'feel' for the action.

All involved believe that the millions of *Grafters* fans will not be disappointed. There is even more to

watch the second time around.

'There are certainly more characters in the second series,' said Sandra Jobling from the Newcastle headquarters of Coastal Productions. The north-east gave life to *Grafters* and she believes that is where the soul of the series still resides, but adds, 'By leaving Newcastle we have been able to explore so many other elements about Joe and Trevor and their relationships with everyone they come in contact with.

'It has been exciting, for we have gone deeper and deeper into their characters as the second series has gone on. With every situation they confronted, there was a way of developing them; they were able to react with more information, more knowledge of the world and of themselves. I know Robson feels he's been able to really get himself entangled in the character and that's a wonderful opportunity for an actor. He and Stephen have been given the space to create.

'Everyone in the cast and crew has been special and because of that we were able to make something special.

'Truly, by the end of the second series audiences will know everything about Trevor and Joe. And they will be surprised.'

STAR QUOTE

'I'm much more a team player than a prima donna'
– Stephen Tompkinson